BUSINESS CORRESPONDENCE 30

THIRD EDITION

Rosemary T. Fruehling, Ph.D.
Manager, Support Services
Division of Vocational-Technical Education
Minnesota State Department of Education
Minneapolis, Minnesota

Sharon Bouchard
Marketing Representative
McGraw-Hill Book Company

GREGG DIVISION/McGRAW-HILL BOOK COMPANY

New York • Atlanta • Dallas • St. Louis • San Francisco • Auckland • Bogotá • Guatemala
Hamburg • Johannesburg • Lisbon • London • Madrid • Mexico • Montreal
New Delhi • Panama • Paris • San Juan • São Paulo • Singapore • Sydney • Tokyo • Toronto

Contents

Illustrations by Barbara Maslin

Business Correspondence/30, Third Edition

6 7 8 9 0   DODO   8 8 7 6 5

ISBN 0-07-022513-3

To the Student

Beautiful Acapulco is the scene for this new edition of *Business Correspondence/30,* and you are invited to join us there!

Join us as we follow Maria Garcia to a Business Correspondence Seminar sponsored by the American Travel Agents Association (ATAA). Maria's company, World Wide Tours, is sending Maria to the seminar to improve her skills in writing business letters, memorandums, and reports. Why? Because writing skills are important for all business workers—especially for Maria, who has just been promoted to senior correspondent for WWT's Word Processing Department.

Read the memo Maria received from WWT's Training and Development Department:

TO:	**Ms. Maria Garcia**	FROM:	**Hazel Rennard**
DEPT:	**Word Processing**	DEPT:	**Training and Development**
SUBJECT:	**Business Correspondence Seminar**	DATE:	**January 4, 19—**

Congratulations, Maria, on your promotion to senior correspondent of Word Processing!

As you know, to prepare you for your new duties, your supervisor, Ms. Jacobs, has arranged for you to attend a special seminar on how to develop effective business messages. This year, I'll be conducting this seminar for the ATAA, and I'm delighted to have you with us.

What you do not know is the location of the seminar. Do you think you can handle Acapulco in March? Would you rather attend a seminar at the Princess Hotel or here in our conference room?

The Princess of course!

Knowing that you'd prefer Acapulco, I have enclosed your tickets and your hotel reservation confirmation. By all means, Maria, we plan to have some fun. But we will also be working hard, for only by practicing can we improve our writing skills

and meet the goals that we have set for ourselves. Specifically, at the conclusion of this seminar, each person will be able to:

1. Understand the important uses of business letters, memos, and reports.
2. Analyze business messages to distinguish between good writing and poor writing.
3. Recognize that good writing is good human relations and that there is no "formula" for good writing.
4. Plan and write each message from the reader's point of view, recognizing that the reader in each case is a human being with interests, wants, and prejudices.
5. Choose among alternatives when solving writing problems.
6. Develop writing craft techniques and apply them by using sentence length effectively, by joining paragraphs skillfully through the use of transitional phrases, and so on.
7. Understand that business writing solves business problems and helps to win and keep customers for the company.

To meet these goals, we have developed the enclosed agenda, which shows the topics we plan to cover during the seminar. Also enclosed is the complete book that we will use to cover these topics—one unit for each topic. You can be sure that we'll give each of these topics our serious attention —even if we do so at poolside!

See you in Acapulco!

HR

/jt
Enclosures
cc Anne Jacobs

Well, your seminar is about to begin, so join Maria and Hazel in sunny Acapulco!

unit 1
PLANNING FOR GOOD WRITING

"Welcome to the American Travel Agents Association's Business Correspondence Seminar!" said Hazel Rennard. "You've read the goals of this seminar (see pages iii–iv), so you know we have a lot of work to do. Let's start right now by reading the following letter from Mr. Daniel Walters of Miller Manufacturing Company."

Dear Ms. Garcia:

There is an error in your August 13 Statement 28311605. You billed my airfare to Sacramento, California, on August 1 as first-class service when in fact it was coach. Attached is a copy of my customer coupon which verifies my coach seat.

I'm concerned with this error on your part, and I am wondering whether or not this has happened in the past. If

it happened during one of my busier travel months, I might not have caught it. Customers depend on their travel agents for good service and efficient billing.

Please investigate this matter and send me a new statement so that I may clear up my account. I am in the process of verifying all my past statements and will be notifying you of any other overbillings and/or overpayments.

Sincerely,

Now respond to Mr. Walters' letter. Upon reviewing the records you find that he is absolutely correct. However, you can see how the problem arose. Mr. Walters was confirmed first class on Flight 50 from Chicago to Sacramento. Walters found he could make an earlier flight out of Chicago that day, so he changed his reservation at O'Hare Airport to Flight 280. Because there was no first-class seat available on this flight, he did indeed fly coach to Sacramento. Write your reply.

WRITING ASSIGNMENT

While Maria is writing her reply to Mr. Walters, let's see how *you* would tackle the assignment. Use the information above in drafting your reply, and then use this space to write your letter.

_____

_____

_____

_____

_____

_____

_____

_____

_____

_____

We'll analyze your letter later. But first, let's read Maria's reply to Mr. Walters. How would you react to this message?

Dear Mr. Walters:

Unfortunately, we were mistaken regarding the correct amount of your airfare from Chicago to Sacramento. It wasn't really our fault, though. If you remember, you were scheduled first class on Flight 50 from Chicago to Sacramento. Looking at your canceled coupon, I noticed that you changed your reservation and flew coach on Flight 280 from O'Hare to Sacramento. How were we supposed to know that you did this? You never told us, and Air Chicago surely didn't tell us.

Customers, too, have a responsibility to their travel agents. Fair is fair. If you would have taken but a few minutes to contact our office, we would not have billed you for first class. In order to prevent such a problem in the future, may I suggest that you alert our agency whenever you change your mind?

Cordially yours,

While reading this message, Maria realized that it certainly would not create a good impression of World Wide Tours. The tone is cold and negative, and it implies that the customer is ignorant and irresponsible. Moreover, even if she had the authority, Maria should never have written this offensive statement: "If you would have taken but a few minutes to contact our office, we would not have billed you for first class."

Maria drafted a second reply to Mr. Walters' letter, but it took a long time for her to complete it. Here is her second letter. How would you react to it if you were Mr. Walters?

Dear Mr. Walters:

Thank you for calling attention to our statement showing first-class rather than coach airfare from O'Hare to Sacra-

mento on August 1. You're right. You owe only $375 for your coach seat.

The trust that customers have in their travel agents is the pulse of the business. You have every right to expect good service and precise billing when you deal with us.

Frankly, there is no good excuse for our not picking up the change in class status from the monthly airline ticket report. When a customer downgrades passage, a notation appears on this report, which is how we are notified about a change. If we had carefully reviewed the report, we would have caught the change and billed you correctly.

You may be assured, Mr. Walters, that the Billing Department has learned to read this monthly airline report much more carefully since this incident, and we are eager to prove it to you.

Please give us an opportunity to serve you again soon. We promise to try to restore your confidence in World Wide Tours in future transactions.

Sincerely,

Maria's second reply creates a much better impression of her travel agency. Mr. Walters may not be completely appeased for being overcharged; however, he probably realizes that it is human to err and that this travel agency intends to improve its customer service. The letter states the correct amount owed, and its tone reflects the writer's sympathy with the customer's problem. It shows that the writer understands the situation and knows her subject as well as the scope of her authority.

Understandably, Maria felt much better about her second letter and decided to use this one to turn in as her first assignment for the Acapulco seminar. But she was concerned over the time it took for her to complete these letters. She knew that she could not afford to spend so much time for every letter she would have to write as senior correspondent in the Word Processing Department!

Fortunately, after Hazel Rennard collected everyone's letter assignment, she discussed the need for planning each message and explained how planning would help the writer not only to create a better letter but also to write it more quickly. Let's listen in.

PLAN AHEAD TO WRITE EFFECTIVE LETTERS

People who are responsible for handling correspondence generally groan at the sight of each day's heap of incoming letters and memos, shuffle through it, and in an effort to get the pile out of the way, start rattling off responses into a dictating machine. Hastily rushing into the writing of business letters, memos, and reports is one of the reasons why so many business messages are unclear, incomplete, confusing, and ineffective. The writers weren't ready to write; they weren't prepared; they didn't plan their messages.

Planning is one of the secrets to good writing. In fact, the need for planning cannot be overstated. Whether you are answering someone else's letter or memo or you are initiating your own correspondence, you will always find it helpful to plan ahead by developing a written working outline. With practice, you will see for yourself that each letter, memo, or report you write will be effective—and will be easier to write—*if you plan ahead*.

No matter what you are writing or to whom you are writing, you should have a plan. This means you will have to think hard about what you want your communication to accomplish. The next step is to organize your ideas in a logical way so that you can achieve this purpose. Let's see how this is done when you are answering a letter; then we'll see how it is done when you are initiating your own correspondence.

Answering Incoming letters. When you answered the incoming letter from Mr. Walters, you had a concrete source of information to consult—his letter. In replying, did you develop a plan or outline so that you could organize your thoughts and ideas? Let's analyze your reply.

1. Does your message assure Mr. Walters that you know your subject well enough to provide him with a complete solution to his problem?
   a. Did you tell him what the correct amount owed is?
   b. Did you include an explanation of the error?
   c. Did the tone of your letter reflect your understanding of the customer's situation?
2. Are the topics you discussed arranged in a forward-moving, smooth-flowing sequence? Although there is not one way to organize topics that are related to a particular subject, whatever method you use should make it easy for Mr. Walters to quickly and accurately follow your thinking.

3. Is your message geared to the needs and interests of Mr. Walters, or could it have been written to almost anyone with equal effectiveness? An effective business communication reflects the writer's total appreciation of the reader as a unique person; it also reflects the writer's understanding of the degree of formality or informality that is appropriate.

4. Does your message indicate that you had a specific purpose in writing? Although some communications have no purpose other than gaining the reader's goodwill, most attempt to sell a product or service, settle a claim, or accomplish a similar objective. A message that has no clearly identifiable purpose represents a waste of time for both the writer and the reader.

5. Does your message make it clear that the reader need not pay the full amount of the statement?

6. Does your message assure Mr. Walters that you know the extent of your authority concerning this matter?

Even if your message was well written, it probably took you more time than you can realistically afford to spend on one letter. An outline—a plan—will help you to save time and to write more effectively if you follow these five steps in developing your outline:

1. State the *purpose* of your letter.

2. Determine what *response,* if any, you would like your reader to make.

3. Decide the main *subject* of your letter and the *topics* related to it that you will have to present and discuss in order to write a complete message. When replying to incoming correspondence, many successful writers simply underline or jot down in the margin the topics that will have to be covered.

4. Decide the best sequence for presenting and discussing the topics you have underlined or listed. After doing this, number or letter the topics in an informal outline; then check to see that each topic is relevant—omit those that are not.

5. Consider your reader and, in every way possible, plan your message from the reader's point of view.

Following these steps, you might have outlined the reply to Mr. Walters like this:

1. *Purpose:* To explain to Mr. Walters that the statement is incorrect.

2. *Response desired:* To have Mr. Walters accept the explanation for the overcharge and to regain his confidence in the service and reliability of World Wide Tours.

3. *Subject:* The coach fare from O'Hare to Sacramento is $375.
   Topics:
   - Changes in customers' passage status are noted on the monthly report.
   - Travel agents should review the report and note the changes in status.
   - There is no good excuse for not picking up the change in class status from the monthly airline ticket report.
   - Customers have a right to expect good service and precise billing from their travel agents.
   - Assure Walters that the Billing Department will be more efficient in reading the monthly report.
   - Convince Walters that he can put his trust in WWT in future transactions.

4. *Best sequence of topics:*
   ① Customers have a right to expect good service and precise billing from their travel agents.
   ② There is no good excuse for not picking up this change in class status from the monthly airline ticket report.
   ③ Changes in customers' passage status are noted on the monthly report.
   ④ Travel agents should review the report and note the changes in status.
   ⑤ Assure Walters that the Billing Department will be more efficient in reading the monthly report.
   ⑥ Convince Walters that he can put his trust in WWT in future transactions.

5. *Consider the reader:* Mr. Walters seems to be a reasonable person who is concerned about an overcharge. As a business worker, he will appreciate the fact that it is human to err. We've got to convince Mr. Walters through our explanation that we carefully analyzed the situation and highlighted the cause of the problem to the appropriate World Wide Tours employees so that such errors will be avoided in the future.

The time that Maria spent in drafting her second reply to Mr. Walters would have been cut drastically if she had prepared such an outline. How much time would *you* have saved?

Initiating Your Own Correspondence.   When you are initiating correspondence, your outline should again include a complete statement of your purpose in writing, the response you want your reader to make, the subject of your message and the topics you will have to present and discuss, and a quick sketch—based on whatever information you can gain from sources that are available to you—of your reader. If you don't personally know your reader or if you have no ready sources of information about your reader—and you often will be writing under such circumstances—there's nothing you can do but use your best judgment in developing a sincere, personal quality.

WRITING ASSIGNMENT

1. In your incoming mail today, you received the following request for a reservation from Evelyn Amoco.

> **Dear Reservation Clerk:**
>
>   **Will you please reserve a double room for me for September 1 to 4. The National Association of Management Personnel is holding a workshop for interested members during that time.**
>
>   **I plan to arrive in New York at 12 noon and check into the hotel before 4 p.m. Please confirm this reservation and quote me a daily rate for a double room.**
>
>   **Since the conference ends at 4 p.m. on September 4 and my plane does not leave until 8 p.m., I want to stay in my room to work until 6 p.m. Please quote me the extra charge for late checkout.**
>
>   **Cordially,**
>
>   **Evelyn Amoco**
>   **Director of Operations**

After checking your reservation lists, you find space available to accommodate Ms. Amoco. Using the following Planning Guide, develop an outline of the points you would have to consider in actually writing the reply.

PLANNING GUIDE

(1) State the *purpose* of your reply.

_____

_____

(2) State the immediate or long-range *response* you want your reader to make.

That she was happy with the prompt Response she recieve from our service.

(3) State the *subject* of your message and list the *topics* that you will have to present and discuss.

Subject: The National Association of Management Workshop.

Topics: That her Reservation will be ready for the days she wanted it for. and just how much it will cost for those days.

(4) Number the *topics* listed above in the order in which you will discuss them.

(5) Give a brief *description* of your reader.

Ms. Amoco know what she wants and she is percise about her schedule as a professional.

2. Using the Planning Guide on the next page, develop a written working outline for *one* of the following letters:

    a. An inquiry about the content of and the one-year subscription rate for *Career Guide,* a monthly magazine published by Smithson Publishing Company.

    b. A request for information regarding admissions procedures and scholarship opportunities at the vocational-technical school or junior college in your area.

    c. A request to a department store in your area for a credit application form and information about payment policies.

      d. A letter asking for a donation from a local business execu-
tive to help sponsor a Careers Day for the senior class in
your school.

PLANNING GUIDE

      (1) State the *purpose* of your message.

*I'm writing this letter to you
to apply For a Credit application.*

      (2) State the immediate or long-range *response* you want your
reader to make.

*I have recieve you letter of interest in
applying for a credit application*

      (3) State the *subject* of your message and list the *topics* that you will
have to present and discuss.

*Subject: Credit Application
Topics: address (2) present Employer
(3) Name of Bank (4.) Credit reFerrenCe
(5.) monthly or Annual interest rate
(6) Thank you for opening a Credit
account with our store.*

      (4) Number the *topics* listed above in the order in which you will
discuss them.

      (5) Give a brief *description* of your reader.

unit 2
PUTTING YOUR IDEAS TO WORK

"You have seen that a good plan ensures a clear message—a message that will have a clear purpose, will cover the essential points or topics, will leave out unnecessary chatter, and will present ideas in a well-organized, sequential way. A plan, therefore, establishes the *general* approach to writing business correspondence. Now let's pay attention to the *specifics*—the sentences that make up the message. Let's see how we can use sentences to present our ideas most effectively."

Hazel Rennard continued: "Remember that you can become highly visible in an organization through your written communication. Bosses expect educated people to be able to express themselves clearly and persuasively. You may not expect to do very much writing, but if you work in a business office, you will have many writing assignments. Whether your work involves accounting, marketing, merchandising, management, secretarial, or clerical duties, written communications will certainly be one of your responsibilities. Don't make the mistake of discovering too late that your writing skills are your greatest asset for promotion and may have a great effect on your career. Remember that your on-the-job business writing represents you and your organization, and your employers will evaluate you by your writing."

WHAT IS BUSINESS WRITING?	Business writing includes any message written for a business purpose. Reports, invoices, itineraries, proposals, memorandums, sales letters, acknowledgment letters, résumés and employment letters—all are business messages. All are intended to communicate information, ideas, statistics, and so on, to other people.

Most of your business writing will involve letters and memorandums. A business letter is written to someone outside the organization, while a memorandum is written to someone inside the organization. Some people call memos *internal communications.* Memos are less formal; they save time, energy, and money.

In a business letter you want to create a favorable impression on your reader; therefore, you use the finest-quality paper you have, printed with an impressive letterhead. The letterhead and high-quality paper will influence the reader favorably regarding you and your business. Keep in mind, however, that good business writing is equally necessary whether you are writing a letter or a memo. After all, when you write a memo to the president of your company, you want to impress upon that person more than anyone else that you are indeed a good writer even though you will use the less costly, timesaving memo form.

Even though letters and memos will probably be your major business writing assignment, you will also be asked to "put your ideas in writing" in the form of reports. Most of the time you will not be told the format of your reports. You will have to determine whether your reports (1) give information, (2) make recommendations, or (3) investigate a subject or topic. Once again, though business reports may differ from letters and memos, all require *good* business writing.

WHAT IS *GOOD* BUSINESS WRITING?	You can be a good business writer if you want to. Probably the most essential ingredient to good business writing is your attitude. First of all you have to want to write well, and this usually comes about if you like your job, know your job, and believe in it. Then

you have to learn to think clearly and to write intelligent sentences. Can you do that?

Business writing is good when it achieves what the writer wants to achieve. Is the message intended to collect money? reprimand a customer for abusing credit privileges? sell an idea to a manager? clarify a company practice? patch up a misunderstanding? win back a customer? Whatever the case, the success of the communication depends upon how well it achieves its purpose.

The best judge of good writing is the reader; therefore, business writing is judged in a human context. It is an individual transaction between a writer and a reader. Thus you won't be able to memorize and apply specific formulas for writing certain "types" of letters. Each transaction demands a personal writing style and an individual response, as people and situations vary. For example, a request written to a very close business friend takes on a different flavor from a request written to the president of a local firm whom you don't know. To illustrate, let's look at the conventional three-step formula for letters of request found in some textbooks: (1) make the request immediately, (2) provide the details, and (3) induce action in the final paragraph.

Now compare the following letters. The requests are identical, but the relationship between the reader and the writer is different in each case—and so is the writing style. Note that the first example follows the three-step writing plan, whereas the second one does not. Would you argue that the second letter is less effective than the first? Doesn't the second letter have a more suitable opening for a communication to a personal acquaintance? As you see, no two human relationships are exactly alike. Therefore, without knowing the nature of a particular relationship, we cannot assume that "rules" will apply in all cases.

Dear Ms. Kailing:

Will you please send me 25 copies of the handout you distributed at your presentation to the Advertising Club on Saturday, August 9? The title of the handout is "How to Stretch Your Advertising Budget."

As you may remember, following your presentation I asked whether I could duplicate your handout for students in my Fundamentals of Advertising class, which starts on September 15, but you kindly offered to send me enough copies for my class.

I certainly appreciate your generous offer, Ms. Kailing. As I mentioned, I would be happy to pay for the cost of these handouts.

Sincerely yours,

Dear Janet:

Your speech was the best presentation at the Advertising Club's all-day seminar last Saturday. I enjoyed it, and I know that everyone else present found your talk as helpful as I did.

Janet, I appreciate your offer to send me 25 copies of your handout, "How to Stretch Your Advertising Budget." Thank you for your thoughtfulness. The students in my Fundamentals of Advertising class will definitely learn much from it.

Class starts on September 15. I'll be sure to share students' comments with you.

Best regards.

Sincerely,

No matter whether you are writing a letter, memo, or report, your ideas must be presented to your reader so that they are understood as you intended them to be. Think about that for a minute. You have learned to develop a plan for good writing and you know what good business writing is. Now you will see how to put your plan—your ideas—to work.

PUTTING YOUR IDEAS INTO SENTENCES

Expressing Ideas in Simple Sentences. In presenting your ideas, you may decide that the best procedure will be to present each of the points in your outline in a separate sentence. For example:

1. Will you please send me information about the admissions procedures for your school.
2. Will you please send me a description of the scholarship opportunities available to high school graduates.

These examples show two ideas expressed in two simple sentences. Since each sentence contains one complete thought only, each can stand alone as an independent idea or an independent clause, as above. However, both sentences can also be combined into *one* complete sentence, as you will see in the discussion below.

Combining Ideas of Equal Importance. Two closely related ideas may be joined into one sentence in a number of different ways. For example, you may prefer to combine two simple sentences by using a comma plus *and*.

1. **Will you please send me information about the admissions procedures for your school, and will you also please send me a description of the scholarship opportunities available to high school graduates.**

The two ideas that were expressed in two simple sentences are now joined by a comma and *and* to form one compound sentence —one sentence with two independent clauses.

The same two ideas may be combined by using a semicolon to join the two independent clauses.

2. **Will you please send me information about the admissions procedures for your school; will you also please send me a description of the scholarship opportunities available to high school graduates.**

In this compound sentence, the independent clauses are joined by a semicolon instead of by a comma plus *and*.

The two ideas expressed in the original simple sentences may be expressed in a third way.

3. **Will you please send me information about the admissions procedures for your school and a description of the scholarship opportunities available to high school graduates.**

Unlike the compound sentences, the new sentence has only one independent clause; yet it combines the same two thoughts that were expressed in the two original simple sentences and in the two compound sentences. The last example contains one subject (*you*) and one verb (*will send*), just as the original simple sentences do. But the last example combines two ideas of equal importance, two requests, by compounding the objects, the things that are requested: "Will you please send me (1) information . . . and (2) a description. . . ."

Considering the alternatives illustrated above, which one do you think is best? Do you agree that the last sentence achieves the writer's objective in the fewest words?

Combining Ideas of Unequal Importance. Suppose you wished to express in one sentence two or more ideas that you felt were closely related but *not* of equal importance. For example, consider the following related ideas:

1. **I am planning to enter college next fall.**
2. **Will you please send me information about the admissions procedures for your school.**
3. **Will you please send me a description of the scholarship opportunities available to high school graduates.**

In this particular case, you may wish to make the first of these ideas subordinate to the other two, because *I am planning to enter college next fall* is not as important to your reader as your requests for the admissions procedures and scholarship information. You may use a variety of devices to make sure that your reader recognizes that this idea is less important. Here are two examples:

1. **Since I am planning to enter college next fall, will you please send me information about the admissions procedures for your school and a description of the scholarship opportunities available to high school graduates.**

The addition of the adverb *since* signals the reader that the first idea is less important than, or subordinate to, the two main ideas that follow. Notice that a comma is used to separate the dependent clause (which expresses the least important idea) from the independent clause (which expresses the main ideas).

2. **Will you please send me information about the admissions procedures for your school and a description of the scholarship opportunities available to high school graduates because I am planning to enter college next fall.**

Notice the use of the adverb *because* to subordinate the minor idea, but in this case, the minor idea is put at the end of the sentence. This position de-emphasizes the subordinate idea further. (If you had positioned the dependent clause *because I am planning to enter college next fall* at the beginning of the sentence—another option—you would have put a comma after *fall.*)

Now consider joining two other ideas of unequal importance:

1. **Mr. Pruett is the acting director of operations.**
2. **Mr. Pruett must approve all expense budgets.**

One of the two ideas, *acting director of operations,* may be subordinated in any of the following ways:

1. **Mr. Pruett, who is the acting director of operations, must approve all expense budgets.**

Note the use of the pronoun *who* to introduce a dependent clause that subordinates the idea of *acting director of operations.* The use of the commas around the subordinate idea makes it clear that this clause provides further information about the subject *Mr. Pruett,* information that is not necessary to either the meaning or the completeness of the sentence.

2. **Mr. Pruett, as acting director of operations, must approve all expense budgets.**

In this case, the preposition *as* introduces a phrase subordinating the idea of *acting director of operations.*

3. **Mr. Pruett, the acting director of operations, must approve all expense budgets.**

The phrase *the acting director of operations* further explains the subject *Mr. Pruett* and is set off by comas because it is unnecessary to the meaning of the sentence. Here the subordinate idea is condensed to an appositive.

4. **Being the acting director of operations, Mr. Pruett must approve all expense budgets.**

The participial phrase *Being the acting director of operations* gives emphasis to the main idea, *Mr. Pruett must approve all expense budgets.*

5. Mr. Pruett, being the acting director of operations, must approve all expense budgets.

Note that here the participial phrase *being the acting director of operations* has less emphasis.

The purpose of this discussion is to illustrate some of the many ways in which you can express your ideas and give them different degrees of emphasis. The more ways that you know how to combine ideas, the better you will be able to add interest and variety to your writing. Clauses, appositives, phrases, and so on, are devices that can be used to subordinate ideas. The more expert you become at using these devices, the better you will write.

WRITING ASSIGNMENT

If necessary, rewrite the following sentences using the techniques of combining ideas.

1. Mr. Smith called you. He wanted to make an appointment.

(1.) He wanted to make an appointment Mr. Smith. (2.) Mr. Smith wanted to make an appointment.

2. You can buy Diamond tires at Steins. You can buy Acme tires at Freemans.

(1.) You can buy Diamond tires at steins, and Acme tires at Freemans.

3. Ms. Carson wrote the article; Mr. Jefferson will edit it.

(1.) Mr. Jefferson will edit the article Ms. Carson wrote. (2.) The Article Ms Carson wrote, Mr. Jefferson will edit it.

4. I look forward to our meeting in March. I hope you will give some thought to the selection of a new agency.

(1.) I hope you will give some thought to the selection of a new Agency, I look Forward to our meeting in March.

5. We congratulate you on the completion of your project. We hope the enclosed description will encourage you to come to Des Moines.

(1) We Congratulate you on the completion of your project; hope the enclosed description will encourage you to come to Des Moines

6. New employees should understand the importance of cooperation. Experienced employees should too.

_____

_____

7. The Federal Reserve bank does not provide service to the general public. It provides service for its members.

(1.) Federal Reserve Bank provide services for it members. not to the general public,

8. Some of our staff members are very experienced. Most of them are trainees.

Most of our staff members are trainees, some of them are very experienced.

9. My instructions were to ship 211 catalogs to Boston, I need to know what has happened to this shipment.

There were 211 catalogs ship to Boston, I need to know what has happened to this shipment.

10. Financial security need no longer be a dream. We hope you will stop in to learn how/our Master Savings Plan can solve your money worries.

(1.) Financial security need no longer be a dream. Our Master Saving plan can solve your money worries, we hope you will stop in to learn how.

_____ **Emphasizing Parts of Ideas.** Both of the following sentences express the same idea, but note that each sentence emphasizes a different part of that idea.

Active

passive

1. Our attorney rejected the contract.
2. The contract was rejected by our attorney.

In the first sentence, the emphasis is on *attorney,* which is the subject of the sentence. The emphasis in the second sentence is on *contract,* the subject of that sentence. In the second sentence, *attorney* is no longer the subject and receives less emphasis.

Obviously, the position of the words in a sentence helps to determine how much emphasis each word receives. But the key to the above sentences is the verb used in each. The first sentence uses the active verb *rejected;* the subject, *attorney,* is performing the action. The second sentence uses the passive verb *was rejected;* the subject; *contract,* receives the action. Your choice of verb determines the emphasis that you will give to various parts of an idea.

By choosing an active or a passive verb, then, you can vary the emphasis on the parts of an idea. Consider this active sentence:

Ms. O'Brien gave Mr. Evans the memo.

Ms. O'Brien is the subject, the doer of the action; *gave* is the action verb; *Mr. Evans* is the indirect object, the person to whom Ms. O'Brien gave the memo; and *memo* is the direct object, the thing that was given.

To change the active sentence above to a passive sentence, do the following:

1. Make either the direct object or the indirect object the subject of the sentence.
2. Use a *being* verb (*am, is, are, was, were, be, been,* or *being*) before the main verb.
3. Use a past participle (a verb form that can be used with *has, have,* or *had*) as the main verb.
4. Use *by* with the subject.

By applying these four steps, you can change the active sentence to either of the following passive sentences:

1. The memo was given to Mr. Evans by Ms. O'Brien.

Note that *memo,* the direct object in the active sentence, is the subject of the passive sentence; the being verb *was* has been used with the past participle *given;* and *by* has been used with *Ms. O'Brien,* the subject or the doer of the action in the active sentence.

2. Mr. Evans was given the memo by Ms. O'Brien.

Mr. Evans, the indirect object in the active sentence, is the subject of this passive sentence. Also note the use of *by* with *Ms. O'Brien.*

Knowing how to create both active and passive sentences will allow you to choose which parts of an idea to emphasize. But unless there is a definite advantage to emphasizing the result or the receiver of an action instead of the doer, you should avoid using passive sentences. Active sentences are generally shorter and more direct.

When stating a formal policy or regulation, however, you may find a passive sentence preferable to an active one. For example: *"Smoking in the stockroom is prohibited."* This passive sentence is more tactful and less antagonizing than an active sentence such as *"I prohibit smoking in the stockroom."*

WRITING ASSIGNMENT

1. Change the following active sentences to passive sentences.

   a. We prefer brief, easy-to-read reports.

Brief easy-to-read Reports are prefer.

   b. The management prohibits smoking in the auditorium.

Smoking in the auditorium or prohibit by management.

   c. The typist should type the manual.

The manual should be type by the typist

   d. You must surrender your credit card to the accounting office immediately.

The accounting office wants you to surrender your credit card immediately. you to surrender your credit card immediately.

e. The manager of our department wrote the following letter to the Acme Supply Company.

The Following letter wrote to Acme Supply Company by the manager of our department.

2. Change the following passive sentences to active sentences.

a. The Krause contract was returned by the file clerk.

The File Clerk returned the Krause Contract.

b. You will be assigned a full-time assistant by the president.

The president assigned you a Full-time assistant

c. A copy will be mailed to you today by my assistant.

My assistant will mail you a copy today

d. The package will be delivered by the messenger before noon.

The messenger will delivered the package before Noon.

e. The letters were transcribed by the secretaries, and the file copies were delivered to the Central Filing Department by a messenger.

The secretaries transcribed the letter, and the messenger delivered the file Copies to the Central Filing Department

f. Carol Bernstein was promoted to assistant manager by Mrs. Harnett.

Mrs. Harnett promoted Carol Bernstein to assistant manager,

g. The attaché case was found in the cafeteria by Elaine Hill
and was returned to its owner by Elaine.

The attaché case that was found in the cafeteria
was returned by Elaine Hill.

Controlling Sentence Length. A knowledge of the techniques
discussed so far will help you control the length of your sentences.
Research indicates that the most readable sentences are 15 to 20
words in length. Naturally, you may have some sentences of 10
words or less and some of 30 words.

Check the average length of your sentences and critically evaluate long sentences. Weigh each word. The busy reader will be annoyed with monotonous, wordy messages that camouflage the real
meaning of your thoughts. In Unit 3, you will learn some techniques that will help you to eliminate unnecessary words and
phrases.

unit 3
USING THE APPROPRIATE LANGUAGE

The members of Maria's small work group decided to have a working lunch around the elegant pool at the Princess. The setting and the delicious food provided just the right atmosphere for the group discussion.

Henry Jenkins, one of the group members, was eager to get to the next topic: appropriate language. Henry said: "So far, so good, but this afternoon's session promises to hit at the main problem in my agency. If Hazel Rennard can teach me how to update some of the phony, old-fashioned, ridiculous expressions that some of our agents dictate, I'll be the company hero when I get back."

As soon as the afternoon session started, Ms. Rennard shared these examples with Maria, Henry, and the other group members. Let's join the group discussion on old-fashioned words and phrases.

OUT OF DATE	UP TO DATE
We desire herewith to bring your attention to a matter of utmost concern to us. From this instance, in accordance with your request and for your information, we have attached herewith our income and expense statement for the year just ended. If you require more information, please call it to my attention subsequent to your review.	**Here is our 19— income and expense statement that you asked for. Please let me know if you need any more information.**

Well, what do you think? Do you agree that the up-to-date version says it better and more clearly? Wouldn't you agree that the first message is overwritten and "a bit much"? Don't you wonder just how today's writers get trapped into sounding so stuffy?

The trouble with using old-fashioned, worn-out language is that the reader doesn't feel personally involved in the human transaction. Instead, the reader feels that the writer mechanically wrote the message without any serious thinking about the ideas that were to be expressed. Words in a language change just like fashions change in dress codes. Think of it this way: Would you dress as your great-grandmother or great-grandfather did? Would you wear high-buttoned shoes or spats anywhere except perhaps to a masquerade party or in a parade? Of course not.

Following are more out-of-date expressions that still crop up in today's letters, memos, and reports. Use the up-to-date replacements to develop a more personal, conversational tone and to make your messages clearer and more direct.

OUT OF DATE	UP TO DATE
I hereby acknowledge receipt of	**Thank you for**

OUT OF DATE	UP TO DATE
Advise	Tell *, preferable*
Are in receipt of	Have
As per our conversation	As *, according to, regrading*
At the present time	Now *, the date, soon*
Enclosed herewith find	Here is *or* here are
I deem	I think
I regret to inform	I am sorry that
In due course	By June 10
In the near future	By next Thursday
Inasmuch as	Since, because
It is my opinion	I believe
Self-addressed envelope	Addressed envelope
Take appropriate action	Act now
Under separate cover	Separately
Up to this writing	Until now
With your kind permission	May I
Your kind favor	Your letter of June 10

"IN" WORDS, CLICHÉS, PHONY WORDS, AND REDUNDANCIES

"In" words or slang expressions are better said than written. For some reason or other, when they are written they make the writer sound childish, immature, and impertinent. Imagine using a greeting like "Hi, boss lady" when writing to your supervisor or telling a complaining customer to "hang it up." "Right on," "nifty," "weird," "no way," "give me five," "hang on," "up front," "tell it like it is," "spaced out," "a real high" may make modern conversation more alive, but such expressions kill writing—especially *business* writing.

The same is true for clichés or overused expressions. Readers get the impression that their writers are lazy, unimaginative, and insincere when they see expressions such as "sharp as a tack," "happy as a lark," "strong as a bull," "an open book," "fast as lightning," "clean as a whistle," "proud as a peacock," "pleased as punch," and so on. An opening sentence such as "I was proud as a peacock to read what you had to say about my speech" seems trite and insincere. Instead, how about "Thank you for your kind remarks about my speech"? It certainly is more conversational and sincere.

Probably the most offensive writing fault is phoniness. Business messages are overwritten when writers exaggerate situations or excessively flatter readers. Exaggerations such as "fabulous meetings," "sensational savings," "terrific offers," "unique opportunities," "dynamic presentations," "unsurpassed performances," and "incredible guarantees" wear out readers by their excess. Flattering statements embarrass and patronize readers. Take, for example, the following statement: "You are to be complimented for making the Tenth Annual Meeting of the Data Processors Association the smashing success that it was. The genius of your keynote address was instrumental to the meeting's success, and only you could have done it." Compliment the reader, but don't overdo it. Instead, say: "On behalf of the members of the DPA, I wish to thank you for making your timely presentation, 'How to Avoid Stress,' the highlight of our annual conference. A speaker knows she has made an impression when other presenters quote her throughout the conference. You were quoted several times in the small-group sessions."

Redundancies are deadwood; they say the same thing over again. Some people say that inexperienced writers tend to repeat themselves because they don't have confidence in their ability to write clearly. For some reason or other the inexperienced writer feels more confident of being understood writing about "two twins" or "new beginners" or "dollar amounts," instead of simply writing "twins," "beginners," or "amounts."

Following are some unnecessary repetitions. Review their replacements and use the replacements instead of the redundant expressions. Learn to watch for redundancies.

REDUNDANT	REPLACEMENT
And etc.	Etc.
At about	About
Both alike	Alike
Check into	Check
Complete monopoly	Monopoly
Continue on	Continue
Cooperate together	Cooperate
Customary practice	Practice
Depreciate in value	Depreciate
During the course of	During
Endorse on the back	Endorse
Final completion	Completion
Lose out	Lose
May perhaps	May
Near to	Near

REDUNDANT	REPLACEMENT
New beginner	Beginner
Over with	Over
Past experience	Experience
Rarely ever	Rarely
Refer back	Refer
Same identical	Identical
Up above	Above

GRAMMAR, PUNCTUA-TION, AND CAPITALI-ZATION

In our language, we depend on word order to convey meaning; in addition, we depend on punctuation and capitalization to make our ideas clear. In Unit 2, we said that one option for expressing two related ideas was to combine the ideas in one sentence by using a comma plus *and:*

Will you please send me information about the admissions procedures for your school, *and* will you please send me a description of the scholarship opportunities available to high school graduates.

The comma before the coordinating conjunction *and* (others are *but, or,* and *nor*) asks the reader to pause after main idea No. 1 so that it can be digested before main idea No. 2. In the example above, the omission of the comma might cause the readers to confuse the equal importance of both ideas. In other words, the comma here indicates that there are two separate and equal ideas. Thus the punctuation serves a definite purpose and helps to make the ideas clearer to the reader. In other cases, capitalization, too, could help to make the ideas clearer. For example, when we write two ideas in two separate sentences, we capitalize the first word of each sentence. The capital letters, therefore, help us to convey the two ideas clearly. For example:

Will you please send me information about the admission procedures for your school. Will you please also send me a description of the scholarship opportunities available to high school graduates.

Whether we approve or not, in our society people judge others by the correctness of their speaking and their writing. Educated people are offended when they see poor grammar, incorrect punctuation, and faulty capitalization. They expect agreement of subjects and verbs, parallel sentence structure, proper subordination of unequal ideas, good word usage, proper verb tenses, and so on. If you need to learn more about such basic grammar principles, begin a self-study project. The reference section of this book is an excellent beginning; however, a complete English grammar program may be your best source for developing good grammar skills. In addition, a comprehensive reference book such as *The Gregg Reference Manual, Fifth Edition,* by William A. Sabin (Gregg Division, McGraw-Hill Book Company), is indispensable to a business writer—even an experienced one. (Ask your teacher for advice.)

WRITING ASSIGNMENT

1. Rewrite the following sentences. Delete outdated expressions, unnecessary repetitions, "in" words, clichés, and phony expressions, and make the appropriate substitutions for any offensive expressions.

   a. We hereby acknowledge receipt of your order and assure you that said order will have the immediate attention of our staff.

   recieve

   We ~~acknowledge receipt~~ of your order, and assure you that order will have the immediate attention of our staff.

   b. I am pleased as punch to tell you that you have been granted an interview on August 3.

   I am please to tell you that you have an interview on August 3.

   c. We tell it like it is, and our nifty prices tell you that our candy sells lower than that of any other candy manufacturer.

   Our Nifty prices tell you that our candy sells lower than that of any other candy manufacturer.

d. We acknowledge receipt of your letter of the most recent date, with reference to the balance of your account in the amount of $750.

(review)

We acknowledge your letter of the most recent date, with reference to the balance of your account in the amount of $750.

e. We have cooperated together and started to commence the necessary processing required to establish the amount of your refund.

We have cooperated and started to commence the necessary processing required to establish the amount of your refund

f. We wish to advise you that unless you remit $77.95 immediately, you can hang it up as far as we are concerned.

We wish to advise you that unless you remit $77.95 immediately, you are finish as far as we are concerned

g. We have finalized arrangements to reestablish your service according to our practice regarding partial payment of unpaid bills.

We have arrangements to reestablish your service according to our practice regarding partial payment of unpaid bill

h. The necessary requirements are that you make remittance by the last day of each month in order to take advantage of a sensational savings plan.

i. Your two fabulous reports are unsurpassed in quality.

Your two fabulous reports are good in quality (well organize and well develop)

j. He takes his customary walks all alone by himself every day.

He takes his customary walks by himself every day

2. The following bank letter does not convey conversational language; uses useless words, unnecessary repetitions, and overworked phrases; and contains grammatical errors. Rewrite the message to make it more effective. Use another sheet of paper if necessary.

Dear Ms. Armstrong:

With reference to the discussion of certain securities of yours now in our possession. We should like to put things up front in order to finalize this matter and get rid of this extra handling and shall clearly do so as soon as you make the first initial move. We have checked into this matter and written to you many times throughout the entire year making suggestions that certain securities be transferred from our name to your name, since you are the beneficiary under Mr. Smith's will. According to our records, from time to time dividend checks come to us in the mail because the securities remain under transfer from our name to your name. You should be fully cognizant of the fact that the stocks to which we make reference are the Silver Oil Company and Purchase Oil and Refinery Company. Due to this fact, and at the earliest possible date, we should be happy as larks if you would bring in the above-mentioned securities, for the specific dividends paid on the stocks can be sent to you instead of being sent to us. A speedy reply from you in the self-addressed envelope would be duly appreciated. You may expect us to respond to your reply as fast as lightning.

Sincerely,

unit 4
KEEPING YOUR READER ON TRACK

Participants in the ATAA seminar came to the next session prepared to do a lot of writing. Maria was especially eager to put to work some of the skills and techniques Ms. Rennard had taught in the first three sessions, and she was given an excellent opportunity to do so when Hazel Rennard assigned the following memorandum as a rewrite project.

Maria reread the rambling memorandum one last time trying to figure out what Harry Steinberg intended. As she read Harry's memorandum, she realized the importance of keeping the reader on track.

Let's read along with her.

TO: **All Employees**   FROM: **Harry Steinberg**
SUBJECT: **London Charters**   DATE: **January 23, 19—**

The sales personnel of the Sunrise Travel Agency are once again thinking ahead, and the difficulty of employees getting an opportunity to move toward higher-level positions or to take advantage of some of the fringe benefits in the form of taking some family trips to faraway places is considered a serious drawback resulting in low personnel morale, a problem which is the concern not only of the personnel manager but of every single employee including the sales manager in charge of the special-priced charter flights to London.

Another problem we have is serious since it is considered unrealistic to make the assumption that every Tom, Dick, and Harry can leave all at one time to take a trip to London, France, Spain, or even Mexico for, say, a week, ten days, or even just for three or four days at a special employee lower-price break and still keep our customers happy by serving their travel needs as they arise. This problem alone has created the most serious problem we have encountered in our desire to please our own people but still keep our market share of the charter business during the best seasons. So you can see that we are baffled as to how we can accomplish our primary and main goal which is to get the morale problem solved before it grows into an even more serious setback. But then how do we keep serving our customers, which is the crux of our income? This is the reason I wrote you this memorandum to tell you that we are trying but that maybe some of you have some ideas of how we can do it on an internal rotation plan—that is, offer you a chance to go to London for only $199, but still keep our usual business doors open to all our customers. Any suggestions will be considered, as we need ideas and help.

First, Maria decides to organize her thoughts and ideas in a written outline, as we learned in Unit 1. She states the *purpose of the memorandum:* Ask employees for ideas on how they might take advantage of the special London charters without disturbing the flow of work during the seasonal charter business. Then she determines the *response she wants to achieve:* Ideas for an employee rotation selection plan. Maria identifies her subject and related topics as follows:

Subject: Employee's Access to London Charters

Topics:
- Need to develop a fair system for allowing employees and their families to take advantage of the London charters.
- Low personnel morale because no such system exists. Employees suggestions for setting up a fair system for taking advantage of the London charters.
- Need to maintain market share of the seasonal charter business while employees travel.
- How to handle the interruption of work flow in the travel agency while employees travel.

Let's leave Maria, as she seems to be heading in the right direction, but let's take her outline and see if we can develop our skills for keeping our reader on track.

READER'S TIME	Harry Steinberg's writing problems include an inability to decide upon the purpose of his memorandum and a failure to develop a good writing plan (these are, of course, serious faults). But it seems that Harry also has another common writing problem. He shows no respect for his readers. He has not constructed his message in a way that would enable his readers to understand the meaning quickly. Will he achieve his purpose for writing the memorandum? Hardly! It took Maria almost 20 minutes to dig through the words to get at the meaning, and she's still not absolutely sure that she knows what Harry *really* means.
SENTENCE LENGTH	Harry's sentences are unclear, incorrect, too long, and poorly constructed. He rambles on and on and traps himself into grammar and usage problems. Consider his first sentence of 90 words:

The sales personnel of the Sunrise Travel Agency is once again thinking ahead, and the difficulty of employee's getting an opportunity to move toward higher-level positions or to take advantage of some of the fringe benefits in the

form of taking some family trips to faraway places is considered a serious drawback resulting in low personnel morale, a problem which is the concern not only of the personnel manager but of every single employee including the sales manager in charge of the special-priced charter flights to London.

Maria adjusted the wording of this "sentence" so that Harry's ideas were easier to grasp.

Because we want all of you to share in our special traveling benefits, we are studying ways in which you and your families may take advantage of charter flights to London.

Although many experienced business writers like to keep their sentences to an average of 20 words, there are no rigid rules as to actual sentence length. If all sentences were of the same length, the reader would soon become bored from the monotony. Some sentences may be 20 words long, others may be under or over 20 words. Some may be 10 or 11 words long, and some may be even 1, 2, or 3 words long. Variety is the key, but it's generally a good rule to shorten sentences longer than 20 words if possible.

Sometimes very long sentences can be made easier to read by breaking thoughts into a list. For example:

The disadvantages of making our charter flights available to employees are that selecting who should go is hard, the work flow of the agency may be interrupted, the employees who can't go may feel left out, and the policy could establish a precedent that may be hard to maintain.

Let's see what can happen when the main ideas in this paragraph are listed as follows:

The disadvantages of making our charter flights available to employees are that:

1. **Selecting who should go is hard.**
2. **The work flow of the agency may be interrupted.**
3. **The employees who can't go may feel left out.**
4. **The policy could establish a precedent that may be hard to maintain.**

Writers often use short sentences such as the following very effectively: *You are right! Hardly! When?*

Subject-verb-object sentences are easy to understand because readers have little opportunity to confuse meaning when the subject begins the sentence. However, too many short sentences make paragraphs choppy, disconnected, and dull. Consider the following memorandum:

TO:	**Esther McCormick**	FROM	**Marianne Pelri**
SUBJECT:	**First Place in Charter Sales**	DATE:	**June 30, 19—**

Congratulations! You did it again. You placed first in charter sales for June. Our agency is flourishing because of you. Try again next month. We will be cheering for you.

WRITING ASSIGNMENT

Rewrite the memo above to change its choppiness. Use a separate sheet of paper.

PARAGRAPH-ING

You have studied techniques of developing sentences that will precisely convey single ideas or combinations of ideas to your reader. Now you are ready to place your sentences in a logical order and group them into paragraphs.

Separate Topics Into Paragraphs. A paragraph may be only one sentence long, but usually a paragraph contains several sentences —all related to the same topic. Thus a paragraph may be defined as a group of sentences closely related to a specific topic.

There are several reasons for paragraphing. Grouping sentences into related topics helps to improve the general attractiveness of your business letter. Your business letter should invite reading; that is, it should *look* easy to read. Wide-enough margins, short- and medium-length paragraphs, tabulated material—all help to make a letter inviting. Long, involved paragraphs are monotonous and forbidding.

The paragraph may also be used to highlight a statement or a question. The technique of enumerating points by paragraphing (treating each point as a separate paragraph) makes it easy for the reader to recognize and answer them.

Join Paragraphs With Transitions.   One of the participants in the ATAA seminar asked Ms. Rennard what she felt was the most important key to writing effective letters and reports. She said, "I grab the reader firmly by the hand, and I hang on until I'm finished." That's good advice. One way to "grab the reader firmly by the hand" and "hang on" is to bridge the gap between paragraphs by using connectors, or transitional expressions.

A good selection of linking words will allow your reader to follow your ideas not only from paragraph to paragraph but also from sentence to sentence. For example, in the following excerpt note how some italicized transitional words join sentences and others join paragraphs.

> **Recent changes in the insurance laws in our state permit insurers to raise the cost of group life insurance coverage. *As a result,* American Mutual Company has announced an increase in its monthly premiums, as shown on the enclosed chart.**
>
> ***However,* this increased cost does not affect any policy currently in effect. It will affect anyone who wishes to increase his or her contributory life insurance policy.**
>
> ***On the other hand,* the cost of medical insurance has decreased for each employee because of our company's excellent record and because the average employee age has decreased within the past five years (due to early retirement). *Further,* the company has now negotiated an inexpensive contributory dental insurance plan, the average cost of which will be about $6 a month for an employee with two dependents. A complete description of this new plan will be distributed early next week.**

Here are some of the common transitional expressions that will help your reader to follow your message:

- **To Show Cause and Effect**

  Accordingly   As a result   Hence   Therefore

  Ms. Holbrook requested that we send copies of the letter to all new managers. *Therefore,* we made 50 extra copies.

- **To Show Exceptions to What Has Been Said**

But	Even though	On the contrary	Otherwise
Conversely	However	On the other hand	Nevertheless

We can, as you suggested, be ready to leave by January 8. *However*, a move at that time will interrupt the children's school schedules.

I agree that Mary is more creative than Laura. *On the other hand*, Mary has no management experience.

- **To Indicate Time, Place, or Order in Relation to What Has Gone Before**

Above all	Finally	In summary	Still
After all	First	Meanwhile	Then
Again	Further	Next	Too

Entering the foreign market is not as simple as it sounds. *First,* there is the language problem. *Then,* there is the matter of finding suitable personnel. *Above all,* we must face up to the fact that we will have to find suitable facilities.

- **To Introduce Examples**

For example	For instance	Namely	That is	Such as

Many departments depend on this service; *for example,* the Accounting Department, the Personnel Department, and the Manufacturing Department.

Don't expect these transitional aids to perform miracles. Remember, if your ideas do not follow a logical sequence, no transitional device will cure your writing. Just as the speaker who rambles on from one thought to another fails to present a clear message to his or her listener, so will you as a writer fail to present a clear message to your reader unless you develop your ideas in a logical sequence and help your reader to follow your message by using transitional expressions.

WRITING ASSIGNMENT

Read the following message. Then place the sentences in logical order and group them into paragraphs. Write the sentence numbers on the lines below. Use one line for each paragraph.

TO:	**Chester Van Buren**	FROM:	**David Jenesen**
SUBJECT:	**Sharing Performance Appraisals With Employees**	DATE:	**August 29, 19—**

    I don't know whether or not we have dollars available for training. Is there any possibility of my arranging for a supervisors' training program next month on performance appraisal? May I hear from you soon so that I can cost out a project proposal. Many supervisors wouldn't share their evaluations with their employees anyway due to three major reasons. They don't want to put themselves in negative situations, as some of the appraisals are bound to be negative. It's a tough enough job telling people what to do. They don't want to be personally blamed for employees perhaps not being promoted or being given raises. The supervisors want to be liked; so they fear that being too honest regarding worker performance may cause employees to dislike them. Most supervisors should take management theory training if for no other reason than to learn the importance of fair appraisal of worker performance.

(1.) Making up a budget for supervisors' training program on performance appraisal. (2) Many supervisors decides against sharing their evaluation with employees because of some negative results. (3) This decision is made in order to keep a good relationship with employees. (4) Most supervisors should take management theory to learn the importance of fair appraisal of worker performance.

THE TAKE-OFF If your takeoff is powerful, forceful, direct, and interesting, your letter may be read carefully. A good way to ensure getting this attention is to open with a short, strong, definite statement. Make your opening short, but make it say something. Why not consider your first sentence of your first short paragraph your headline? Don't be afraid to have only two or three short sentences in your first paragraph. Actually, the fewer the better. In sales letters, the first paragraph is designed specifically to attract attention.

    Remember that any reference to the date or to details of previous correspondence should be placed in a subordinate position. In other words, "Your January 12 letter was received yesterday" places the date of the previous correspondence in a predominant position; "Thank you for your letter of January 12 requesting 12 reams of our No. 16 white mimeograph paper" places the *thank you* and the actual sale in the predominant position and the date in the subordinate position.

You will ensure a powerful takeoff if you can describe action that was taken on your reader's behalf. This is always the most effective opening to a business communication. Action is impressive because it implies decision, and all of us are favorably impressed when our requests have been met. Note in the following examples how action in favor of the reader gets each message off the ground.

Dear Miss Strauss:

Enclosed is our book, *Preparing for College*, which you requested in your letter of June 12. You will be pleased to know that this book is free to all high school Merit Scholarship winners.

Dear Mr. Yamato:

Thank you for inquiring about the possibility of becoming our sales representative in the Midwest. Every one of us in the Minneapolis office feels that you would make an excellent addition to our marketing team.

Another way to ensure strength and power in your opening sentence or paragraph is to avoid the use of participial expressions, except to subordinate an idea. Inexperienced writers who frequently use participial expressions may produce grammatically incorrect sentences. Notice how easily the following lengthy participial expression could be mistakenly considered a complete sentence: "Having reviewed your application for employment as a secretarial trainee." It is not, of course, a complete sentence.

Avoid all unnecessary preliminaries in your first sentence, and don't rehash what your reader already knows. For example, "Your order of January 10 reached my desk today" is obviously unnecessary. The reader realizes that you would not be responding if the order had not reached you, so why rehash?

Remember that the first sentence and the first paragraph are extremely important. Everything that follows builds from this opening. Be natural, and be yourself. Do not begin the first paragraph with the old-fashioned, pompous wordiness of yesteryear. Compare the following examples.

OUT OF DATE	UP TO DATE
We desire herewith to acknowledge receipt of your letter of June 10. Heretofore, in the future, we wish to inform you that it will be unnecessary for you to notify us directly. From this instant it is with pleasure that we announce that notification of late payments may be made to the respective agent in your city.	**Thank you for your letter of June 10 notifying us of your late payment. For your convenience, all future notifications of late payments may be made directly to your agent, Mr. T. Jones.**

Obviously, the natural, up-to-date version is easier to read as well as easier to write. The first message is excessive; it marks the writer as pompous and behind the times. Acting natural and saying things as you would in a cordial conversation will get your letter off the ground with a powerful takeoff.

THE LANDING

The landing, the last paragraph of your letter, should have a definite purpose. It should make it as easy as possible for the reader to take action or to accept what you have written. If you have considered your reader's point of view from the first word of your letter to the last, the reader will see how easy it is to do what you ask and how it will benefit him or her to do so. By enclosing an addressed envelope or postcard, you may readily stimulate action.

One of the serious errors that writers make is to ramble, and the last paragraph seems to be the frequent place for such rambling. Inexperienced writers are sometimes confused about how to end a letter. If your message has been conveyed, make a smooth landing. The reader doesn't expect you to be flowery or chatty. Just end the letter. And don't say, "A speedy reply will be appreciated"!

The most ineffective of all closings is the participial ending. Ending your letter with, for example, "Trusting we shall hear from you soon" is weak and inconsequential. "Thanking you in advance" is even worse; it violates two rules of good letter writing. First, it is a participial expression; it should not be used as an independent sentence. Second, it is presumptuous because it assumes that the reader will grant what you ask.

Compare the "rough landings" on the left with the "smooth landings" on the right.

Looking forward to hearing from you soon, we are

May we hear from you soon.

Hoping that you will place your order with us soon

Enclosed is an addressed, postcard for ease in ordering.

Trusting you will give this matter your immediate consideration

Will you please act promptly on this request.

By providing your reader with a powerful takeoff (a good opening paragraph) and a smooth landing (an effective closing paragraph), you will almost ensure that your reader's journey through your message will be a pleasant one.

THE BEST APPROACH

Although you have been given some suggestions for making an impact in your opening and closing paragraphs, there is really no "best" approach or formula. As already emphasized, so much depends upon the relationship between you, the writer, and your reader.

WRITING ASSIGNMENT

1. Rewrite the following ineffective opening sentences and paragraphs.

   a. In regard to the equipment, it is being shipped from New York today addressed to you at your office and have somebody there to receive the shipment because it must be signed for and will you be sure to acknowledge by letter to me.

   Please have someone sign for the equipment from New York. If their are any problems, please write to me about it.

   b. In reply to your letter of July 1, we wish to advise you that an examination of our records shows that your policy is still in force.

---

c. Acknowledging receipt of your letter of January 10 in which you asked for a copy of *Good Listening*. We are glad to send you this copy.

_____

_____

2. Correct the following ineffective closing sentences and paragraphs, or indicate when an unnecessary one has been used.

a. Hoping it will be possible for you to give us your decision on this matter by Friday, we are,

_____

_____

b. Assuring you in advance of our appreciation for your kind attention and hoping that we may have the opportunity to do the same.

_____

_____

c. Hoping you will return your broken glasses for credit as soon as possible.

_____

_____

3. You are a correspondent in the credit section of a department store to which Carol Zanna has applied for a charge account. You are writing to an officer of the bank where Miss Zanna has a checking account. You want to know Miss Zanna's credit rating. Write your opening paragraph—and remember that this is a routine inquiry, since you do not know Miss Zanna personally.

_____

_____

_____

_____

_____

4. You are writing a letter to Mr. Mark Pulaski, the personnel director of the Power-O-Peat Company, Seattle, Washington, to apply for the position of accounting trainee. You state your experience and qualifications. You know that he will be attending a convention in your hometown, Spokane. It would be very convenient if you could have an interview with him sometime during his stay in Spokane. Write your final paragraph, your request for action.

_____

_____

_____

_____

_____

unit 5
PSYCHING YOURSELF TO GET THE RESULTS YOU WANT

Maria's rewrite of the Harry Steinberg memorandum was singled out as the best planned and organized revision. This was no surprise to Hazel Rennard, because Maria's writing was improving rapidly each day. However, what was surprising to Hazel was that Maria's revision of the Steinberg memorandum also reflected excellent *tone*. Her memo considered the *reader's* point of view.

Since the topic for the next 8:30 a.m. session was "Getting Results From Your Communications," Hazel used Maria's rewrite to illustrate the quality of reader-directed messages. She said, "Listen to the tone of Maria's opening sentences." Then she read Maria's rewritten version.

Because we want all of you to share in our special traveling benefit packages, we are studying ways in which you and your families may take advantage of our charter flights to London. We need your help, though! Since we must figure out a way to continue to provide first-class service to our customers during a period of high-volume sales, we thought we would ask for your suggestions.

In your day-to-day involvement, you are in the best position to make recommendations concerning the following system problems: (1) Since not more than three employees should be gone at one time, who would be given priority? (2) What kind of temporary help would be available to handle the work load of those employees who are gone? (3) How can we handle requests from employees who have used up their vacation days but still would like to take advantage of the London charters? (4) Would you anticipate any morale problems with employees who are not able to go?

Compare the tone of Maria's rewrite with Harry Steinberg's pompous message: "The sales personnel of the Sunrise Travel Agency are once again thinking ahead. . . ." (Giving oneself a pat on the back is usually offensive.) ". . . employees getting an opportunity to move toward higher-level positions or to take advantage of some of the fringe benefits in the form of taking some family trips to faraway places is considered a serious drawback resulting in low personnel morale. . . ." (The insinuation that a trip to London will make up for weak career opportunities could make some employees feel that they are being "talked down" to.) "Another problem we have is serious since it is considered unrealistic to make the assumption that every Tom, Dick, and Harry can leave all at one time to take a trip to London. . . ." (A person likes to be treated as an individual, not a "Tom, Dick, or Harry.")

Maria courteously chose words like "share in our special traveling benefit packages" to make her employees feel part of a close family relationship. Also, by saying, "We need your help," Maria cemented the feeling of teamwork in solving common problems.

When she said, "In your day-to-day involvement," she made the employees feel important.

DEVELOP A FEEL FOR YOUR READER	As a beginning writer, you should try to develop the skill that Maria has learned—thinking about your reader rather than yourself when writing. This quality is instrumental in achieving the results you want. It is not easy, though, unless you genuinely appreciate the need to get and keep as many good customers as possible. If you can genuinely feel that you can do your job best by creating and maintaining good human relationships inside and outside the organization, you will succeed in considering your reader all-important.

Please and *thank you* are words that suggest courtesy, but these words do not automatically ensure a proper display of respect, concern, consideration, and helpfulness. The intangible qualities of courtesy can best be achieved if you will remember that all correspondence must be written from the reader's point of view. The reader's point of view is really the "you" attitude or seeing things through the reader's eyes.

"I want to get a part-time selling job with your firm so that I may earn money to enroll at the University this fall" is certainly not considering the reader's point of view or using the "you" attitude.

"Will you please consider me for the part-time selling vacancy in your firm. I plan to attend the University this fall and need to earn money to pay for my college expenses" incorporates the word *please* and the word *you.* However, it still lacks the intangible qualities of courtesy which show that the reader's point of view has been considered.

Let us try to change the paragraph not only by adding a courteous *please* and using the word *you* but also by considering the reader. "Will you please consider my application for the part-time sales position with your firm. Since I plan to major in marketing and merchandising at the University this fall, you can be sure that I would be an enthusiastic trainee, eager to learn selling." A prospective employer will certainly be more impressed with the last illustration, because the writer has indicated how he or she would be an asset to the employer's firm.

To write effective communications, then, consider the reader's point of view. Always assume that your reader is a successful, extremely busy business executive—not too busy, however, to recognize the benefits or profits of hiring a promising applicant or sending the materials requested or replacing a defective product.

Unfortunately, you cannot inject the "you" attitude into your letters merely by substituting *you* and *your* for *I* and *we*, *my* and *our*, and so on. Consider the following two examples and notice that there is no magic in simply saying *you*, *you*, *you*.

Dear Mr. Isbjörn:

I'm sorry for the delay in sending you your confirmation for Northwest Flight 292 to Hawaii on October 12 at 2 a.m. Because I have been unable to reach you by telephone and because I want to make sure I send you exactly what you want, I'm holding your tickets until I get more information.

Just indicate on the enclosed card what class service you want; then mail it to me today. As soon as I receive the card, I will send you your confirmation. I'm happy to say that Flight 292 is on a DC-10 with many seats still available.

Sincerely,

Dear Mr. Isbjörn:

You failed to tell me what class service you wanted on Northwest Flight 292 to Hawaii. As a result, you will not be able to have confirmed reservations until you send me further information.

Will you please let me know exactly what class service you want. You may expect your confirmed tickets only after you send me this information.

Sincerely,

Do you see that the writer of the first letter psyched himself to get results?

RESPOND PROMPTLY Hazel Rennard spent a good portion of one afternoon session emphasizing the need to respond to letters and memos quickly. She said: "Probably one of the most serious complaints made about employees in business is that they fail to answer their correspondence within a reasonable period of time. This infuriates customers and clients because they feel that they are being ignored. As a business writer, you may be wise to consider the common business motto: 'Answer in 48 hours.' No matter how great your writing skills are, you can 'blow it all' by letting your communications go unanswered for too long."

Timeliness in answering correspondence is an important technique for you to learn as you develop writing skills. A successful correspondent is well organized, so let's see if we can help you to develop a process for responding to your incoming mail.

1. Sort through your mail several times a day to make sure that priority mail gets your attention first.
2. Divide the mail into two groups, higher-priority items and lower-priority items, based on the urgency of each message.
3. Respond to higher-priority mail first. Even if you don't have all the information at hand to answer the questions or problems, acknowledge the letter and tell the reader when a reply can be made. For example:

Dear Mr. Bouchay:

Your request for information regarding our annual home show exhibit will be sent to you as soon as my boss, David Renee, returns from a month's business trip to Heidelberg, Germany.

He will make the decision upon his arrival on Thursday, May 15, at which time I will send you the information you need.

Recognize that in some instances a too-prompt reply is discourteous. For example, responses to requests for credit by poor-risk applicants who must be told "no" or requests for employment by persons lacking the necessary qualifications shouldn't be written too quickly. Obviously, in these situations, a fast "no" may convince applicants that their requests were handled hastily. In such instances, it may be wise to wait a week to ten days before responding.

WRITING ASSIGNMENT

Rewrite the following "I" attitude sentences so that they have a considerate "you" quality.

1. I wish to apply for the position of stenographer as advertised in yesterday's *New York Times*.

_____

_____

2. I am particularly eager to join your company, Ms. Levitt, because I know of its reputation for promoting promising employees.

_____

_____

3. Our company wishes to announce our Grand Opening.

_____

_____

4. We wish to call attention to the fact that we are in the sheet metal business in this city with a ten-year record of service. We are in a position to give good service, and we will be glad to give an estimate anytime.

_____

_____

5. In reply to your inquiry of August 2, this is to say that our *Sales Technique Bulletin* will not be reprinted, so we cannot send a copy at this time. Sorry.

_____

_____

6. We cannot quote you a price until we have seen what specifications are needed.

_____

_____

**SAY IT
SIMPLY**

Another important consideration is to say just enough and to say it as simply as possible. As already stated, this means omitting redundant, old-fashioned words and phrases, which contribute to making messages long and pompous, and replacing "in" words and clichés.

Remember to say just enough to achieve the purpose of your message. When you have done this, you have attained unity and organization. Most letters don't need to be longer than one page, and you can often cut about a third of a message and not destroy its meaning. Be careful, though, not to cut so much that your message appears choppy and incomplete.

Undoubtedly, Mr. Isbjörn would have been furious with the travel agent who wrote the following message because it substitutes brevity for completeness.

Dear Mr. Isbjörn:

We can't send you your confirmation and are thus canceling your reservation.

Sincerely,

**DEVELOP
THE APPRO-
PRIATE
TONE**

"It's not always *what* you say—it's *how* you say it," and in no other case will this be more true than in business letter writing. Yes "*how* you say it" expresses your personality and that of your company. Your friendly nature, your helpful manner, your radiant personality, and your courteous gestures must be reflected through the *positive* tone of your messages. Since we have already discussed the importance of considering the reader, we have laid the groundwork necessary for an understanding of how to develop the appropriate tone.

Once you have realized the importance of the "you" attitude and have mastered its use, your messages will be sincere, courteous, direct, and honest rather than sharp, blunt, overbearing, and pompous. Only when the reader's point of view is foremost in your mind and in your writing will your messages be pleasant, persuasive, convincing, and positive.

Many of your business letters will be written to arouse interest or to move the reader to action. Therefore, they must appeal to basic wants.

Illustrated below are examples of a letter written to arouse the reader's interest and a letter written to move the reader to action.

Dear Reader:

Why are so many young adults like you joining the swing to SUPER, the magazine for today's sophisticated young adults?

It's simple—we know modern teens have a wide range of interests, and we try to keep you posted on all of them. But we don't tell you how to think. We just present the latest facts, the newest happenings . . . and let you make up your own mind!

SUPER is lively, colorful, exciting. And now you can have it sent to you personally at HALF-PRICE.

See for yourself why the smart set is swinging over to SUPER. Get 18 big issues (a full year and a half) for only $9.00! Detach and mail the postpaid card today—we'll bill you later.

Sincerely,

Dear Ms. Harris:

Your account shows a balance due of $486.22 for dental work completed during January and February. It is now April, and you still have not paid for these dental services.

By paying in full now, Ms. Harris, you will maintain the excellent credit rating that you now enjoy and you will help us to meet our commitments.

A stamped, addressed envelope is enclosed for your convenience in mailing us your check for $486.22.

Sincerely,

Notice the vivid tone of the words used in the sales letter—*young adults, swinging, sophisticated, lively, colorful, exciting, smart set.* Note, too, how the sales letter has built an emotional appeal to teenagers based on their desire for identity with the "swinging set." Notice how the persuasive words of the collection letter—*maintain the excellent credit rating that you now enjoy, help us to meet our commitments—*

have also built an appeal, a psychological appeal to Ms. Harris to maintain her good image and to be fair.

ACCENT THE POSITIVE

One of the best ways to tone up your letters is to accent the positive or pleasant features and to downplay the negative or unpleasant features. Your readers will be critical of the letters they receive. They will avoid those letters that are pessimistic, negative, and unpleasant but will seek out those that are optimistic, positive, and pleasant. Positive language stresses the light rather than the dark side. Positive language emphasizes what can be done and leaves what cannot be done to implication.

Observe how the following pessimistic or negative sentences reveal an unpleasant tone. Then notice how the tone is improved in the optimistic or positive comparisons.

NEGATIVE	POSITIVE
We are sorry, but we cannot extend more than $300 worth of credit to you.	**You can buy up to $300 worth of merchandise on credit.**
You failed to state what size you wanted; therefore, we cannot send you the shoes.	**You will receive your Scarpa shoes within three days if you send us your shoe size on the enclosed card today.**
We cannot allow you to exchange this garment because it has been worn.	**If this garment had been returned before you wore it, we would have gladly exchanged it for you.**
We cannot deliver on Saturdays.	**Deliveries are made Monday through Friday only.**

The tone of *sorry, failed,* and *cannot* is negative and unpleasant. Notice how the first sentence takes a negative situation and makes it positive when it is changed from *we cannot extend* to *you can buy up to $300.* In the second and third sentences, conditional words like *if* and *would* are used to transform a negative message into a positive message. And the last sentence is negative with an active verb but is positive with a passive verb!

Goodwill is an intangible quality that is extremely important to the success of a business. In order to have the goodwill of others, you must, of course, show goodwill in all your dealings. One way to do so is to accent the positive features of each situation.

WRITING ASSIGNMENT

1. Rewrite the following negative sentences.

   a. We can't refund your $38 because you did not return the article within ten days of purchase.

   _____

   _____

   b. You're only 18 years of age. We do not grant credit to minors.

   _____

   _____

   c. We are sorry to say that you cannot have 75 copies of *Sailing*.

   _____

   _____

   d. We regret that your slides arrived in unsatisfactory condition.

   _____

   _____

   e. We do not sell running shoes.

   _____

   _____

   f. You neglected to send us your shoe size. How can we send you your order?

   _____

   _____

   g. Your account of $7.50 is past due.

   _____

   _____

h. How can you afford to hurt your credit rating? It's shaky now.

_____

_____

2. Rewrite the following letter to improve its tone by stressing the positive aspects of a negative situation.

Dear Mr. Rodgers:

You must have been disappointed and angry to have your running shoes arrive after the New York Marathon. We deeply regret this unfortunate occurrence because we know you were probably going to wear the shoes to run in the race. It's no wonder that you were mad. I would have been too.

We were out of your size when your order came in. Unfortunately, we neglected to notify you so that you could have bought them from one of our other stores. We can't mail running shoes from one of our other stores unless a deposit is made, and you didn't make a deposit. Then we got so busy we just didn't have time to follow up on your order.

Cordially,

_____

_____

_____

_____

_____

_____

_____

_____

_____

_____

_____

_____

unit 6
CHOOSING THE RIGHT FORMAT

Communications that *sound* good should also *look* good. Business letters, memorandums, and reports should achieve a "total look" about them, just as clothing styles do. The reader should never be distracted from the ideas of the writer; therefore, the format of a message should not distract the reader—it should not draw the reader's attention away from the content of the message.

The letter, memorandum, or report format should tell the reader something positive about the writer and the organization represented. The reader forms an initial impression from the appearance of a business communication, and this impression has a long-lasting effect. The effect influences the way the reader will receive the message.

Hazel Rennard will very briefly review correct format for communications because Maria and all the others attending the Acapulco seminar already know the preferred format for letters, memos, and reports for their organizations. Beginning writers, however, need to learn the different formats available for dressing up their business communications to achieve the "total look."

LETTERHEAD AND STATIONERY	The letterhead and stationery you use for your business communications should be simple and in good taste. The writer doesn't want the message to appear too loud, too busy, or too eye-catching or the positive "total look" will be lost.

The most common size of stationery is referred to as standard size. It measures 8 ½ by 11 inches and is usually white or an off shade of white. A good-quality bond paper should be used. The first sheet usually displays a professionally designed, printed letterhead, which includes the name of the company, its address (with ZIP Code), and its telephone number (with area code). The design of the letterhead may also include a trademark or logo (a company symbol). As a new worker, you will probably have little to say about the selection of the letterhead style; however, experienced office workers may help make key decisions regarding the revision of letterheads.

A letterhead is never used for second sheets, and occasionally continuation pages are necessary (see page 149). The second sheet, though plain, should match the quality and color of the letterhead stock. A heading for second sheets usually includes the addressee's full name and courtesy title, the date, and the page number blocked at the left margin; for example:

Mr. George Wallace
October 12, 19—
Page 2

Or, depending on the letter style, the heading may be centered, as follows:

Mr. George Wallace   **2**   **October 12, 19—**

It is considered poor taste to use company stationery to write personal business letters, such as letters applying for jobs or letters asking others for recommendations. For such letters, plain, good-quality, standard-size paper should be used, and a three-line heading (called a *return address*) should be typed which includes the writer's street address; city, state, and ZIP Code; and a date line.

119 Hunter Avenue
Nashville, TN 37210
June 15, 19—

This return address is typed in block style either at the left margin or at the center of the page, depending on the letter style used. Note that the writer's name is not included in the return address; as we will see, it is included at the end of the letter in the complimentary closing.

ENVELOPES

Envelopes should match the size, quality, and color of the letterhead paper. This is seldom a problem, because most businesses order both their letterhead and their envelopes from the same supplier at the same time. The return address is usually printed in the left-hand corner of the envelope, and the writer's name is typed above the return address.

For personal business letters, where the use of company stationery would be in poor taste, the envelope should be plain and match the paper in size, quality, and color. The writer's name and full address should be block-typed in three lines in the upper left-hand corner of the envelope.

Because of the emphasis on highly sophisticated word processing equipment, window envelopes are becoming very popular. You may find this to be true in your new job. The letter is folded so that the inside address of the letter shows through the window, thereby serving as the envelope address. Obviously, the window envelope eliminates the need to type an address on an envelope.

LETTER PARTS

The parts of a business letter include:

1. The company's letterhead or the writer's return address
2. The date line
3. The reader's name and address
4. The salutation (the greeting)
5. The body (the message)
6. The complimentary closing (the good-bye)
7. The writer's signature

8. The typed signature

9. The typist's reference initials and any notations.

Each of these parts is explained below and illustrated on the model letters shown on pages 62–65.

1. *The company's letterhead or the writer's return address* has already been discussed. Examples of printed letterheads are shown on pages 62–65; a typed return address is shown on page 58.

2. *The date line* includes the month (spelled out), the day, and the year, given in this order: *September 6, 19 —*. Whether it is typed on letterhead stationery or on plain stationery, the date line is generally positioned so that it falls about 2 ½ inches (or 15 line spaces) from the top of standard 8 ½- by 11-inch paper. On letterhead stationery, the date line is usually typed three lines below the end of the letterhead. On plain paper, of course, the date line is included in the return address, as you have already seen.

3. *The reader's name and address* gives the name and address of the person to whom you are writing. If the letter is sent to a person's home, only the person's name and complete address (street address, city, state, and ZIP Code) are included. However, if the letter is sent to someone's business address, the person'a name and business title and the company's name and complete address (street address, city, state, and ZIP Code) are included. In all cases, a title such as *Mr., Mrs., Ms., Miss,* or *Dr.* must precede the reader's name.

4. *The salutation* is typed at the left margin on the second line below the reader's address. Traditionally, *Dear* is used before the person's name, such as *Dear Miss Abernathy* and *Dear Ms. Edward,* or in more familiar relationships, *Dear Henry* and *Dear Bette.* In recent years the use of *Ms.* has become widespread. Some women, regardless of their marital status, prefer to be called *Ms.,* while others prefer *Miss* or *Mrs.* In order to avoid embarrassing situations, try to find out what the woman's preference is by referring to previous correspondence. The use of *Gentlemen* when writing to a firm or organization has been under serious attack in recent years. An alternative to *Gentlemen* is *Ladies and Gentlemen,* which is by no means widely accepted at this time.

5. *The body* or message of your communication is single-spaced with double spacing between paragraphs. Paragraphs may be blocked at the left margin or indented five spaces.

6. *The complimentary closing,* traditionally the "good-bye" line of the letter, is typed on the second space below the body of the letter. Depending on the letter style, it is either blocked at the left margin or typed at the center of the paper. The most popular closings today are *Cordially yours* and *Sincerely yours.* For a more personal tone, when using a salutation such as *Dear Henry* or *Dear Bette,* the *yours* can be dropped; *Cordially* and *Sincerely* stand alone. The formal *Yours very truly, Very truly yours,* and *Very cordially yours* are rarely used because of their extreme formality.

7. *The writer's signature* is handwritten and appears between the complimentary closing and the typed signature.

8. *The typed signature,* with the writer's business title (typed on the same line or directly below it, depending upon length), is blocked four spaces under the complimentary closing. The titles *Ms., Mrs.,* and *Miss* are used only to show a woman's preference for one courtesy title. The title *Mr.* is used only when a man's name could also be a woman's name—for example, with names such as *Lynn, Carroll,* and *Pat.* For some reason or other, some business writers have developed a practice of not using a typed signature line, leaving the reader with the problem of deciphering the correct spelling of the writer's name. This practice should be avoided.

9. *The reference initials, carbon copy, and enclosure notations* follow the typed signature line. The current practice is to include lowercase typist's initials only: for example, *kmp.* In the past, when the writer did not use a typed signature, the initials of the dictator were typed in capitals followed by a colon or slash and the typist's initials: *JTL/kmp,* for example. With the typed signature line, however, it is redundant to type the dictator's initials. The reader obviously knows the writer's initials from the typed signature line. If the writer is also the typist of the letter, no initials need to be used. This is the clue that the writer is also the typist.

Following the reference initials, enclosure notations are used, if appropriate. The word *Enclosure* or the abbreviation *Enc.* is typed at the left margin on the line below the reference initials. To indicate more than one enclosure, an arabic number is typed after the notation: *Enclosures 2* or *Enc. 2,* for example. The enclosure notation is a valuable addition, for not only does it remind the sender to include the items to be enclosed, but it also signals the receiver to look for them in the envelope.

The notation *cc* is typed one space below the enclosure notation (if one is used) or one space below the typed signature line (if no enclosure notation is used). The *cc* notation stands for "carbon copy" and means that a copy of the letter has been sent to the person or persons whose name or names follow the *cc* notation.

LETTER AND PUNCTUA-TION STYLES	Most companies use one basic letter and punctuation style, and all the people in the company use it. Some companies, however, leave the selection of letter and punctuation style to the writer and/or typist.

The four letter styles illustrated on pages 62 through 65 are the acceptable formats for business letters. Of these, the full-blocked and the blocked letter styles are probably the most popularly used formats.

Two punctuation styles used for business letters are the standard style and the open style. The standard style requires the traditional use of a colon after the salutation and a comma after the complimentary closing. The open style omits this colon and comma. The open style is illustrated in the full-blocked letter (page 62) and the simplified letter (page 65), where it is always used. The standard punctuation style is illustrated in the blocked letter (page 63) and the semiblocked letter style (page 64).

MEMORAN-DUMS	Messages sent within a company are typed on memorandum forms. Reports, requests, acknowledgements, and many other internal communications are prepared on a convenient form similar to the one illustrated on page 66.

The stationery on which memorandums are typed has a printed heading that includes four major categories, identified by these guide words: *TO, FROM, SUBJECT,* and *DATE*. In larger companies, in order to speed up delivery, other categories may be added, such as *DEPARTMENT, FLOOR,* or *BRANCH*.

The receiver's name appears after *TO*, generally without a courtesy title such as *Mr.* or *Ms.* The writer's name is typed after the word *FROM;* no courtesy title is used before the writer's name.

SUBJECT identifies at a glance what the message is about. It should be worded so that it is short and to the point. The current date is typed after the word *DATE*.

The body or message of the memo, like the body or message of a letter, is single-spaced with an extra space between paragraphs. The body of the memorandum starts on the third or fourth line below the last line of the printed heading. The paragraphs in

office services corporation
200 s. wacker
chicago, illinois 60606
telephone: (312) 555-1399

March 6, 19--

Ms. Andrea S. Rodgers
Director of Personnel
Glendale Insurance Co.
500 Bannister Road
Kansas City, Missouri 64131

Dear Ms. Rodgers

Subject: Form of a Full-Blocked Letter

This letter is set up in the full-blocked style, in which
every line begins at the left margin. A few companies modify
it by moving the date to the right, but most firms use it as
shown here. Because this style is the fastest to type, it is
considered very modern. It is natural, although not necessary,
to use "open" punctuation with this style of letter.

This letter also illustrates one arrangement of the subject
line, which may be used with any style of letter. Like an
attention line, a subject line may be underscored or it may
be typed in capital letters. In a full-blocked letter, it
must be blocked; in other letter styles, it may be blocked or
centered. The subject line usually appears after the salutation and before the body, for it is considered a part of the
body. (In a simplified letter, the subject line is used in
place of the salutation.)

Legal firms and the legal departments of companies sometimes
prefer to use the Latin terms Re or In Re instead of the
English word Subject.

Yours very sincerely

Pauline E. Campbell
National Sales Manager

The full-blocked letter style is considered modern and functional because all
copy starts at the left margin. Note the subject line and open punctuation style.

office services corporation
200 s. wacker
chicago, illinois 60606
telephone: (312) 555-1399

March 6, 19--

Mr. George Kirsch, Manager
Word Processing Department
Central Children's Hospital
100 W. 39th Street
Philadelphia, Pennsylvania 19104

Dear Mr. Kirsch:

In business letters, we generally display quotations and
similar special data in a special paragraph, like this:

> The paragraph is indented five spaces on both
> sides and is preceded and followed by one blank
> line space.
>
> If it is necessary to use more paragraphs for the
> quotation, then a standard single blank line is
> left between paragraphs.

We indicate the mail service (a space below the enclosure
notation, if used, or on the line below the reference initial)
only if we are sending the correspondence by some special
service, such as "special delivery" or "registered"; and we
do so only to get the fact indicated on our file copy of the
correspondence.

                         Yours very sincerely,

                         Pauline E. Campbell
                         National Sales Manager

PEC/jn

REGISTERED

P.S. We treat postscripts in the same way that we treat other
paragraphs, except that we precede each postscript by "PS:"
or "P.S."

In the blocked letter style, the date line and the complimentary closing are indented, as well as any displayed paragraphs. All other lines begin at the left margin. Note the postscript and the special mailing notation.

NATIONWIDE office services corporation
200 s. wacker
chicago, illinois 60606
telephone: (312) 555-1399

March 6, 19--

Excelsior Hotels, Inc.
100 King Street West
Toronto, Ontario
M5H 1B7

ATTENTION CUSTOMER RELATIONS MANAGER

Gentlemen:

     For a letter design that is both distinctive and yet
standard, try this style: semiblocked (one of the two most
popular styles) with the paragraphs indented five spaces.

     This letter shows you an attention line typed in all-
capital letters. It may also be typed in capital and small
letters, with the complete line underscored. In two regards,
however, the use of the attention line is standard: It is
accompanied by a "standard" salutation, such as "Gentlemen,"
"Mesdames," "Ladies," or "Ladies and Gentlemen"; and it is
typed <u>above</u> the salutation.

     Worth noting also in this letter are the following:
(1) the use of "standard" punctuation, which calls for a
colon after the salutation and a comma after the complimentary closing; and (2) the use of the "cc" notation at the
bottom to indicate to whom carbon copies of the letter are
being sent.

            Yours very truly,

            Pauline E. Campbell
            National Sales Manager

PEC/jn
cc Ms J. Lambeau
   Dr. H. Moon

All paragraphs are indented five spaces in the semiblocked letter style. Note the
attention line and the "cc" notation in this letter.

NATIONWIDE office services corporation
200 s. wacker
chicago, illinois 60606
telephone: (312) 555-1399

March 6, 19--

Mr. Stanley K. Chan
Elmwood & Chan, Brokers
2000 Wisconsin Avenue NW
Washington, DC 20007

THE SIMPLIFIED LETTER

You will be interested to know, Mr. Chan, that several years
ago the Administrative Management Society designed a new
letter form called the "Simplified Letter." This is a sample.

1. It uses the full-blocked form and "open" punctuation.

2. It contains no salutation or closing. (AMS believes such
    expressions to be meaningless.)

3. It displays a subject line in all capitals, both preceded
    and followed by two blank lines. Note that the word
    "Subject" is omitted.

4. It identifies the signer by an all-capitals line that is
    preceded by at least four blank lines and followed by
    one--if further notations are used.

5. It seeks to maintain a brisk but friendly tone, partly by
    using the addressee's name at least in the first sentence.

Perhaps, Mr. Chan, as some say, this form does not really
look like a business letter; but its efficiency suggest that
this style is worth a trial, especially where output must be
increased.

PAULINE E. CAMPBELL
NATIONAL SALES MANAGER

To many business writers, the simplified letter is cold because it does not have a
salutation and a complimentary closing. Like the full-blocked letter, it is an efficient style: all copy starts at the left margin.

MEMORANDUM

THOMPSON INDUSTRIES INC.

To:	Carol B. Newton	**From:**	Jack Cornwallis
Dept.:	Marketing	**Dept.:**	Product Development
Subject:	Product Training Sessions, January-June 19--	**Date:**	July 9, 19--

As you requested, I have developed a tentative schedule for product training sessions for the first six months of next year.

January	14-16	Rochester, New York
	28-30	New York, New York
February	18-20	Los Angeles, California
	25-27	San Francisco, California
March	10-12	Chicago, Illinois
April	14-16	Houston, Texas
		Dallas, Texas
May	19-21	Kansas City, Kansas

This schedule reflects the increased need for training in areas where we now have many inexperienced sales representatives-- namely, in New York, California, Illinois, Texas, and Kansas. In these states, we now have a total of 30 sales representatives who have been with our firm two years or less. Thus I suggest that we focus our training sessions for the January-June period in these five states. As usual, each session is scheduled for three field days. I am sending a copy of this suggested schedule to each of our regional managers, to make sure there is no conflict with other activities they may have planned for their representatives.

Please let me know whether you have any comments on this proposed schedule.

                                        JC

jn
cc: Regional Managers

The guide words *To, From, Subject,* and *Date* are printed on memorandum forms to simplify the typist's work. This form also includes the guide word *Dept.* in each column.

1

memorandums are usually blocked at the left margin to save typing time. This left margin is set two or three spaces after the longest guide word. (For example, in the illustration on page 66, *SUBJECT* is the longest guide word; therefore, the margin is set two spaces after the word *SUBJECT*.) The right margin is set to equal the left margin.

To avoid the need for second pages, some writers prefer to align the left margin with the printed guide words. When this is done, the right margin should be extended to balance the left margin.

A signature may or may not be used. Some writers prefer to initial their memorandums either at the bottom of the memorandum or next to their typed name, which follows the guide word *FROM*.

WRITING ASSIGNMENT

1. Type the following letter from George L. Holloway to Dr. Shirley R. Adzick in proper letter form. Dr. Adzick is the president of Adzick Management Consultants, Rochester, New York 14623. Use the letter and punctuation style of your choice. Assume that you are using letterhead stationery. Use today's date.

   Dear Shirley:

   As I suspected, your agenda for your July 2 workshop on communications and human relations is indeed complete. This makes our job extremely easy to do on this end. The topics for each of the four sessions sound very good to me. I agree with you. We will have no difficulty in providing two overhead projectors and two screens so that you will be well equipped for your sessions. As soon as we receive your vita and publicity photo, we shall use them in our promotion work here. I am somewhat doubtful whether I will be able to attend the NBEA meetings in Chicago due to additional responsibilities I have taken on here at the University. In the meantime, however, if there are any questions involving our workshop, please let me know. Before July 2, I hope to see you at the Walton Golf Tournament. It has been a really rough winter, and all of us are looking forward to spending as much time as possible out-of-doors. Cordially, George L. Holloway, Department Chairman

2. The following message from David Jones is to be sent to all employees regarding legislative wrap-up. Type the memo on a separate sheet of paper. Create your own heading.

The 19— Omnibus School Aids Bill contained few changes for secondary and adult vocational education. However, considerable changes were made in the laws governing post-secondary vocational education. The following are some major points contained in the legislation. As soon as a final copy of the bill is available, we will send it to you. *Secondary.* (1) A deficit appropriation was made for FY 19— in order to maintain a 50 percent support rate. (2) The vocational handicapped percentage increased from 50 percent to 70 percent. *Post-Secondary.* (1) A limit of $150,000 was placed on transfer from the general fund to the capital fund. However, a transfer for remodeling was allowed up to $50,000. (2) Student memberships will be counted on a quarterly rather than a daily basis, and membership adjustments must be made quarterly. (3) An extended attendance time of up to 10 percent was allowed for handicapped and disadvantaged students.

unit 7
WRITING EVERYDAY "PLEASE SEND ME" LETTERS

At the business writing seminar in Acapulco, all the attendees, including Maria, could not help feeling that Hazel Rennard was moving rapidly toward reaching the goals she had established at her first session. All the participants were very pleased with their personal accomplishments and progress in developing business writing skills. The background information that had been presented so far was in just the right dosages, for the writing assignments were becoming easier and faster to write.

Maria couldn't suppress a smile as she thought, "Anne Jacobs knew exactly what she was doing when she sent me to this conference." Hazel had told Maria that she and Anne, the chief executive of World Wide Tours, had been college friends at Texas State, both majoring in journalism. No wonder Anne Jacobs was a stickler about promoting a good image for WWT through good written communications!

Maria was beginning to feel very good about herself and her new job as senior correspondent of World Wide Tours when she heard Hazel say: "Let's get started, writers. We have two days left before we leave this lovely city and hotel, and I want you to write all types of business letters before we depart."

EVERYDAY REQUEST

"Let's begin this day by talking about and then writing one of the most common types of letters—the 'please send me' letter. Simple, everyday letters asking for information, materials, favors, appointments, or reservations should be a snap for you to write. Although these requests are not difficult to write, you should remember that they, too, must be well written if they are to achieve their purpose." Then Hazel Rennard made the following points regarding "asking" letters. Make sure you incorporate her suggestions in your writing.

In writing routine "asking" letters, your most important responsibility will be to include all the information the reader will need to fill your request. It is always wise to keep your request as brief as possible, but not at the expense of sounding discourteous or omitting important details. An incomplete request will force your reader to write back to you for more information. This is annoying and unnecessary.

Sometimes it will even be to your advantage to enclose a stamped, addressed envelope so that your reader can answer your request more easily. Whether you do or not, of course, it is always essential to include your return address on the letter itself. This rule of courtesy is often violated when the request is personal and a letterhead is not used. For some reason or other, the writer often types the date line only. This practice forces the reader to have to staple the envelope (which usually includes a return address) onto the letter. Remember that if you consider the situation from the reader's point of view, you will include all necessary information in your request.

Requesting Materials. When asking for free material, make sure that you have a clear mental picture of what you want and that you convey this same clear picture to your reader. Whenever possible, address your request for materials to a particular individual. Sometimes, doing so may require extra effort on your part, such as making a telephone call to the company. If it is impractical to obtain the individual's name, write to the specific department handling your request. For example, if you are asking a firm for a description of its employee benefits, you should address your request to the personnel department; if you are asking for advertising literature, you should address your request to the advertising department; and so on.

A letter requesting free materials is usually brief and easy to write. Obviously, because the materials have been offered free, the writer is in a position to get what he or she asks for. A strong, persuasive plea is not necessary. Even though these letters are easy to write, good writers use these as opportunities to practice good writing (they're just more comfortable doing so). Writers know that they get good at their craft only by doing lots and lots of writing, so they take advantage of every opportunity to use their skills.

For routine request letters, good writers should maintain a courteous attitude. For example, it is courteous and shows good common sense to indicate how you intend to reimburse your reader for any mailing costs involved, and it is presumptuous to request several copies without assuming some cost for mailing. If only one copy of a pamphlet or other item is requested, a stamped, addressed envelope may sufficiently cover the mailing cost.

Look at the following example of a request for free materials:

Ladies and Gentlemen:

Will you please send me your current catalog and price list. I am in charge of our company's reference library and receive requests from our employees for office supplies and equipment catalogs.

May I be put on your mailing list so that I may receive updated catalogs as they come out?

Cordially yours,

Notice that this letter contains all the information that the reader will need to respond favorably to the request. It is short, to the point, contains all the information needed for the reader to respond, and yet it is courteous.

The writer should be commended for not making the usual beginner's mistake of thanking the reader in advance. It is presumptuous for a writer to use the same letter both to make a request and to thank the reader. Since the writer is asking for something, it seems only courteous to allow the reader the privilege of saying "yes" or "no." A message of gratitude should be extended only after the request has been granted.

Compare the following letter asking for the same free materials:

Ladies and Gentlemen:

Please send me your latest catalog.

Cordially yours,

This letter is clear enough. It certainly is short. The "please" is courteous, but the letter is brusque. More careful planning on the part of the writer might have him or her consider the following points: How can I keep getting the new catalogs and avoid writing for new ones? How can I prevent the company from sending a sales representative out now when we really don't need to see one?

WRITING ASSIGNMENT

Assume you are employed by the Jennings Manufacturing Company, 232 Washington Avenue, Minneapolis, MN 55401. Write to the Meredith Management Consultants, 2385 Baymiller Street, Hamilton, OH 45012, for 75 copies of their free instructional pamphlet, *Avoid Stress Situations,* used to train marketing, editorial, and management personnel to cope with everyday pressures. You wish to have these pamphlets by January 9, in time for distribution at a national conference from January 10 to 13.

_____

_____

_____

_____

_____

_____

_____

_____

_____

_____

_____

_____

_____ **Requesting Information.**   Letters requesting information vary depending upon how general or how specific the request is. In some cases you may not be exactly sure of what you want or of what the reader has that you can use. What you are doing, in effect, is asking the reader to come up with some suggestions that will help you.

In such situations, you must state your problem specifically. And be reasonable. Don't ask for the moon and expect to get it! Imagine someone sending IBM, Xerox, or the 3M Company the following request: "I am interested in word processing. Will you send me everything you have in your file about word processing." Such requests for "all there is" about computers, selling techniques, and so on, are unreasonable and probably will not be filled.

Read the following excerpt from a request made to a postage meter company:

> **Beginning next fall, our Training Department will offer a "How to Give a Speech" course to employees. For this course, we would like to videotape each participant and play back his or her presentation, allowing participants to see themselves as they appear to the audience. We are interested in using your Flex-16 videotape equipment for this purpose.**
>
> **Will you please answer the following questions on the Flex-16:**
> 1. **Is Flex-16 available on a rental basis? If so, what is the monthly rental cost? Is there a minimum term for renting?**
> 2. **Is Flex-16 available for sale? Is so, what is the complete selling price?**
> 3. **If we were to purchase the Flex-16, what warranties would we receive? Is a separate service contract available, and if so, how much does the contract cost?**

4. **For playback, can the Flex-16 be attached to any standard television set?**
5. **Must any special lighting equipment be purchased for use with the Flex-16?**
6. **Does the Flex-16 lens have telescopic features?**

This example is effective because it is specific. Notice how the writer itemized each question, making it easier for the reader to understand the request. Also notice that the questions asked are brief and within reason and that they allow the reader to organize the answers. Instead of including the trite expression "We shall appreciate your reply as soon as possible," the writer assumed that the reader would give this request prompt attention. Obviously, the writer had no deadline; otherwise, he or she would have asked for the information by a definite time.

WRITING ASSIGNMENT

You plan to enroll at the University of South Florida this fall but are unsure of what procedure to follow. Write a letter to the University of South Florida, Tampa, Florida 33620, requesting information about admissions procedures.

_____

_____

_____

_____

_____

_____

_____

Requesting Reservations.   Most people make hotel reservations by telephone, especially for those hotels which have toll-free telephone numbers. It is wise, however, to write a letter requesting a hotel reservation. The letter provides a record for you and tells the hotel to mail you a written confirmation. In any event, when either telephoning or writing for such a reservation, you should request a written confirmation. If you have ever gone to a hotel and found that there was no record of your reservation, you will appreciate the importance of getting a written confirmation!

When writing for reservations, be sure to include the exact arrival date and any late afternoon or evening arrival information. If you are a member of a group attending a convention, be sure to mention that fact in your letter because you may be entitled to a special rate. Consider the following hotel reservation request:

> **Will you please reserve a single room with shower for Mr. Dan Wheeler for Friday, October 16. Because of a late flight, Mr. Wheeler will check in around 10 p.m.**
>
> **Mr. Wheeler will be attending the Data Processing Workshop at your hotel on October 17 and will check out on that morning.**
>
> **Please confirm this reservation before October 5.**

The hotel reservation clerk will quickly read and understand this message. If a room is available, Mr. Wheeler will get it.

WRITING ASSIGNMENT

Request a reservation for a single room for yourself at the Heath Hotel, 1200 Avenue of the Americas, New York, New York 10020, for three nights. You will arrive on May 16 and depart on May 19. Be sure to confirm the $42-a-day room rate.

_____

_____

_____

_____

_____

_____

_____

_____

_____

SPECIAL REQUESTS	**Requesting Favors or Approval Through Memorandums.** Requests made within a business firm for approval or favors are typed on memo forms. Sometimes a request from one employee to another is made orally; however, if the request requires the spending of money or is complex, it should be stated in writing, even if it has been discussed beforehand. The request should be stated in writing so that the specific details of the request—and any reply to it—are on file for the record. The request should also be in writing so that the person to whom you are writing can get further approval if necessary. Consider the following memo:

TO: **L. Joe Cotton**   FROM: **Betty Shuster**
SUBJECT: **Accounting Seminar**   DATE: **May 13, 19—**

The attached brochure describes the 23rd Annual Accounting Seminar to be held in Birmingham, Alabama, from July 14 to 20. It looks like a good program, and I would like to attend.

Notice the sessions on developing five-year plans for comptrollers. As you are aware, I will be faced with this job shortly, and I can certainly use any information I can get to improve my Management-by-Objectives program. I estimate my expenses will be about $250, including air transportation. My assistant, David Bringall, will be able to handle my responsibilities while I am away.

The writer has given her supervisor enough information so that if necessary he can take it to his superior. By including the brochure, she has given Mr. Cotton an opportunity to evaluate the reasonableness of her request. The tone is convincing and is appropriate for writing to a supervisor who may have to ask for further approval.

WRITING ASSIGNMENT

Write a memo to your supervisor (use your teacher's name) requesting permission to take two extra days off in June (the 7th and 8th—Thursday and Friday) to attend the wedding of your cousin in Boston, Massachusetts. You are to be in the bridal party, and you have some last-minute things to do, including attending the wedding rehearsal. You have a long trip to Boston ahead of you.

TO: FROM:

SUBJECT: DATE:

_____

_____

_____

_____

_____

_____

_____

_____

_____

_____

_____

_____

Following Up Requests. Many people fail to respond to requests made of them; therefore, they need to be written to *again*. Whatever the reasons why readers do not respond (they're too busy, they've fallen behind in their work, they don't want to answer), writers gain nothing by writing a "mad" follow-up. Consider the tone of the following letter written to request information a second time.

> **Ladies and Gentlemen:**
>
> **I just don't understand why you didn't respond to my request for a copy of your latest catalog. You won't get orders from us until we get one (we've already placed several orders with your competition).**
>
> **Maybe you'll take time to send me one this time. I hope so.**

Wow! The writer's anger—and rudeness—shows all over the place. Statements such as "I don't understand," "you won't get any orders," and "Maybe you'll take time" sound childishly rude. A person receiving such a request may deliberately delay sending the catalog!

WRITING ASSIGNMENT

On March 15, you wrote to all department managers asking them for their budget needs for the second six months of 19—. It is now April 10 and several budgets still have not been sent to you. Your total budget package needs to be submitted to the president by April 15. Using the following memo form, write a second request to your department managers.

TO: FROM:

SUBJECT: DATE:

_____

_____

_____

_____

_____

_____

_____

_____

_____

_____

Requesting a Speaker.   Letters that ask someone to give a speech are more persuasive than the other "please send me" letters we have discussed. Even though speakers usually charge fees for their work, good speakers are in great demand and, therefore, are very busy. Sometimes the fee that can be offered hardly covers expenses. For these reasons, a persuasive letter must be written which emphasizes the importance of the audience or function and why the speaker was chosen. Obviously, such letters must be courteous, complete, and convincing.

WRITING ASSIGNMENT

You are program director of the Mid-Continent Guidance Counselors' Meeting, which holds its yearly meeting at Southwest College on September 21, 19—, at St. Joseph, Missouri. The theme of this year's conference is "How to Motivate Students," and you are looking for a speaker—one who can open the meeting.

Ms. Elizabeth Rathmill, 4335 Everett East, Wayzata, MN 55391, is a well-known motivational speaker, and you are to write to her asking her if she will accept the invitation. Remember to be friendly and persuasive, and don't forget to include all the basic information Ms. Rathmill needs to either accept or refuse the invitation.

_____

_____

_____

_____

_____

_____

_____

_____

_____

_____

_____

_____

_____

_____

unit 8

ANSWERING REQUESTS AND WRITING THANK YOU'S

"Recent studies show that the most common letter written in business is the one that answers a request of some kind. It is only courteous to respond to a request, be it positive or negative, on the day that it is received."

Maria understood that Hazel was once again emphasizing the need for the writer's concern of the reader's point of view. But, Maria wondered, just how realistic is it to try to answer all request letters on the day they are received? Maria was just about ready to ask Hazel about the practicality of her comment when she remembered the discussion regarding setting priorities and quickly following up requests that couldn't be answered on the same day by writing a short note telling the reader when an answer could be expected.

RESPONDING TO SIMPLE, GENERAL REQUESTS

Some companies use routine form letters when responding to requests that are simple and general. They feel it isn't necessary to take time to write a personal message when confirming a reservation, filling an order, or sending free materials. Within the last ten years, however, more and more businesses are trying to display a more personal image to their customers and clients. Because of this trend, many companies are saying that they want every request, even those that are simple and general, to be answered by personal letter. Since businesses spend millions of dollars each year on direct-mail selling and advertising in order to attract requests, orders, or customer/client interest, it makes good sense to treat customers individually rather than routinely.

Let's consider a response that was made to a request to hold a conference at the Palm Springs Hotel:

Dear Ms. Van Tries:

Thank you for thinking about the Palm Springs Hotel for your national sales conference from May 29 to 31. We are pleased to tell you that we can serve you, and we would appreciate the opportunity to host this special event.

The enclosed brochure will give you the information you requested. You will be happy to know, I am sure, that we have decided to offer you our special off-season rates normally not given until after June 1.

Just last week we hosted the National Association of Women Amateur Golfers at our hotel. The chairwoman, Nancy Watson, told us that our 18-hole golf course was one of the finest in California. Along with our well-cared-for golf course, our hotel has nine clay tennis courts and two Olympic-size pools. All these facilities are lighted for evening use and are available to conference attendees and their families without charge.

Our sales conference manager, Joseph Burke, is especially effective at sitting down with you and your planning team to help you determine which of our 25 meeting rooms (equipped to handle both small- and large-group settings) will best serve your conference needs.

We hope that you choose the Palm Springs Hotel for this special occasion. I have asked Mr. Burke to hold accommodations for the dates you have requested. If you will confirm your reservations by March 30, I'll tell him to call you so that he can meet with you to get your plans underway.

Sincerely,

Do you agree that the tone of the letter is personal and persuasive? Doesn't it appear that the Palm Springs Hotel is honored to have been considered the site for an event as special as a national sales conference? Do you think that the reader will feel that the request was treated personally rather than routinely? How about the last sentence? Do you think the writer was pushy, or do you think that the writer is wise in asking for action?

Or do you think that the reader would be more impressed with the routine form letter which follows?

Dear Customer:

Thank you for requesting information about the Palm Springs Hotel. Enclosed is a brochure that will give you the information that you requested.

WRITING ASSIGNMENT

1. Respond to this simple, general request for materials. You are employed by Meredith Management Consultants, 2385 Baymiller Street, Hamilton, Ohio 45012. Mrs. Suzanne Devito, sales manager of the Jennings Manufacturing Company, 232 Washington Avenue, Minneapolis, Minnesota 55401, has requested 75 copies of your instructional pamphlet *Avoiding Stress Situations*. She needs these copies by January 9. You have had excellent reviews of this pamphlet by other business firms. You find, however, that you can spare only 15 copies now, for the

supply is running low and will not be replenished until after January 9. Write a letter of response to Mrs. Devito.

_____

_____

_____

_____

_____

_____

_____

_____

_____

_____

_____

_____

RESPONDING TO SPECIFIC, COMPLEX REQUESTS

Requests that are highly specific require a more complex response. Specific requests could not be answered with a general form letter; therefore, all require a personal response. An important rule to follow when writing your replies to such requests is to be courteous and prompt. Another important consideration is to be sure that your responses are complete. Do they include all the information that has been requested? If several questions are asked, you can help your reader by answering each question in a separate paragraph or by enumerating them. If all your answers are positive, number them in the same order in which they are made. However, if they are not all positive, you may have to change the order of the responses to minimize the negative ones. In other words, start with your positive responses and end with your negative responses.

Assume you have received the following request:

> **To handle our monthly volume of letters more efficiently, we should like to buy or rent a postage meter machine. Since we now mail approximately 500 letters a month, we are interested in your P-36 model.**

Will you please answer the following questions about your P-36 model machine? Do you sell this machine? If so, what is its complete selling price? Do you rent this machine? If so, what is the monthly rental cost? Does this machine print a short advertisement as it meters envelopes? Does this machine seal envelopes?

Consider the following response made in paragraph form:

Thank you for your interest in the Randolph Speedy Mailers. You will enjoy reading the enclosed brochure, which describes our P-36 model in detail.

It is to your advantage to purchase the P-36 Speedy Mailer on a rental-purchase plan. This plan allows you to make rental payments with an option to buy.

As indicated in the enclosed brochure, businesses with a monthly volume of 500 letters "sing the praises" of the Randolph Speedy Mailers.

You will be pleased to know that the P-36 Speedy Mailer prints an advertisement and meters the envelopes in one simple operation (see page 8). It also seals the envelopes with ease and speed (see page 9).

This letter is specific, and the paragraphs make it relatively easy for the reader to follow and respond to the message. Now consider this response in enumerated form:

Thank you for your interest in the Randolph Speedy Mailers. You will enjoy reading the enclosed brochure, which describes our P-36 model and answers your questions in detail.

1. You may buy the P-36 Speedy Mailer, but it is to your advantage to rent this machine with an option to buy.
2. The rental charge is only $75 a month. The cost of the meter is, of course, proportionate to the amount of postage used (see page 8).
3. The P-36 Speedy Mailer prints a small advertisement as it meters envelopes—all in one simple operation (see pages 8–9).
4. The P-36 Speedy Mailer also seals each envelope automatically.

If you have more questions—or if you'd like to see a demonstration of the Speedy Mailer in operation—please call our representative in your area, Connie Wiener, at 555-1234. She will be happy to make an appointment at your convenience.

This letter is more specific than the previous example and makes it easier for the reader to respond because it uses more concise enumerations.

Answering Yes. Answering yes to a specific, complex request naturally has a high reader interest. For example, if the shipment can be made exactly to the customer's specifications, this news alone will be good news and should be told immediately and with enthusiasm. Less important things such as when the order was received, details of packing, and payment arrangements should be included, but they should be placed in subordinate positions. Consider the following three samples:

1. **We were pleased to receive your order, and it will be shipped today.**
2. **Your order was shipped today, and you should receive it soon.**
3. **Your Order 236 should arrive on Tuesday, June 25, as we shipped it airmail today.**

Notice how the third example considers the reader by telling her the good news. She is not left worrying about whether or not she will get the order. Once you have enthusiastically given the good news, you may then proceed to discuss the other details— practical aspects such as when the order was received, packing and payment arrangements, and so on. Perhaps the following example will clarify this discussion.

Your order for 10 Durable blueprint files should reach you on Monday, June 12, as we shipped it by truck yesterday. Our Invoice B172-04 totaling $504.50 ($47.95 per file plus $25 for delivery) was charged to your regular account, No. 415-657, as you requested in your order of May 30.

Do you see how this message gets off to a good start and still brings in the practical details? You may notice that the writer has not said thank you, even though this is an excellent opportunity to show appreciation for the order. Although the reader is more interested in the good news of positive action, you should by all means show your appreciation in the letter—but show it after you have indicated action. Be careful, of course, to avoid trite expressions such as "Much obliged for your order" or "Welcome to our family of charge customers." Sometimes the tone of your letter will be the only thing necessary to indicate your appreciation.

WRITING ASSIGNMENT

Using the opening paragraph of a letter from the Durable File Company (on page 85), complete the letter. Follow these suggestions: Show appreciation without being gushy, welcome your new customer, resell your product, and end your letter with a friendly comment that will build goodwill.

_____

_____

_____

_____

_____

_____

_____

_____

_____

_____

_____

Analyze your letter using the following checklist; write *Yes* or *No* next to each question. Be objective in your analysis!

_____ **a.** Is your letter direct and reader-oriented? Did you avoid wishy-washy chatter like "We received your order and were happy to fill it"?

_____ **b.** Did you include the practical details; for example, description of goods and method of payment?

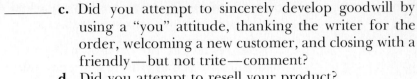

_____ **c.** Did you attempt to sincerely develop goodwill by using a "you" attitude, thanking the writer for the order, welcoming a new customer, and closing with a friendly—but not trite—comment?

_____ **d.** Did you attempt to resell your product?

If you answered "yes" to all the questions on the checklist, you can be sure that your letter will receive an enthusiastic welcome and that you have handled this special order with care.

_____ **Answering Maybe.** Acknowledging a complete and specific special order with positive action is much easier and more pleasant than acknowledging an incomplete order. When you receive an incomplete order, you may be annoyed by the inconvenience and the delay caused by the writer's oversight. You must minimize the unfortunate results of incomplete orders to avoid embarrassing the writer and to get the information neeeded to complete the order.

It is not necessary to trace the oversight step by step; in fact, it probably does not have to be stated at all, merely implied. Putting the reader on the spot is antagonizing. Just as indefensible is the apologetic manner of blaming yourself for not being able to understand the order. Your primary concern should be to get the information necessary to complete the order. This is the only way to handle this negative situation.

Remember that any chatty opening, if you use such an approach, should be brief and sincere and should set the stage for the negative message. Avoid overusing negative words. One effective opening is to refer to the desirability of the product. The opening could also refer to the actual order and indicate appreciation for the order.

Consider the following example:

Dear Miss DiAngelo:

You will be pleased with the modern, clean, general appearance of your correspondence when you use the variety of type-style elements available for your new Manning electric typewriter. Thank you for your October 15 c.o.d. parcel post order for four electric, nickel type elements.

So that you can get exactly the type style you wish, will you please review the enclosed catalog and make a selec-

tion. **As you will notice, we have marked in red those styles which have been the most popular.**

After reviewing the catalog, will you please check your selections on the enclosed stamped, addressed order card and mail it to us today. Upon receipt of this card, we will mail your four electric type-style elements immediately, as all models are in stock.

Sincerely,

This letter does a good job because it does not criticize the customer for not providing sufficient information to fill her order. The opening paragraph restates the desirability of the product. The next paragraph invites the reader to make a selection. The final, friendly note makes it easy for the reader to reply and is positive and not stereotyped like "A speedy reply would be greatly appreciated."

Answering No. Not all replies can say yes or merely ask for more information. Some replies must refuse readers' requests. Like the letter asking for more information, the letter or memo that says no to a request is negative in nature—more negative than an acknowledgment of an incomplete request. Therefore, refusals are difficult to write. However, even when you cannot supply all the answers or all the data requested, you can always offer some help or make some positive suggestion to maintain the reader's goodwill. Remember that every piece of correspondence must be courteous and should help create goodwill; but this is especially true of refusals.

Successful refusals begin on a positive note—never on a negative note! The reasons for the refusal should be developed logically so that the reader will understand that the refusal was not made on mere whim. And the refusal itself should be stated in a positive manner.

WRITING ASSIGNMENT

The staff of *Hi-Lite* (a school newspaper) is attempting to pay part of its publication costs by selling leather and ceramic handicraft made by the students. The secretary of the staff has written a letter to your employer, who is the vice president of the Towers Department Store at the Tremont Plaza Shopping Center, requesting one of the store windows to display these goods from April 1 to 14. Towers Department Store has a company policy that only store merchandise can be displayed in its windows, and your employer lacks authority to change company policy. Write a reply for your employer. Your employer takes great pride in the schools in the community and in no way wants to reflect a sorehead, unenthusiastic attitude. However, the request *cannot* be granted.

_____

_____

_____

_____

_____

_____

_____

_____

_____

_____

_____

_____

_____

An analysis of your answers to the following questions will help you judge the effectiveness of your communication.

1. Did you begin your letter with a stereotyped, obvious beginning such as "Your letter of March 4 has been referred to me for a reply"?
2. Did you convey a negative tone? Did you avoid giving reasons for the refusal?
3. Did you present your reasons at a time in the letter when they were unimportant because the reader was already dejected by the brusque refusal? For example, did you say something like "Many requests are made for the use of our windows for dis-

play, and unfortunately all requests cannot be met. Therefore, to avoid any partiality, we must refuse all who ask"?

4. Did you hide behind company policy as in "Due to company policy, we will be unable to allow you to display your handicraft in our windows"?

5. Did you then remind your reader of the disappointment by adding "We hope that you will understand our reasons for refusing our display windows for your leather and ceramic handicraft"?

6. Did you end your letter with a trite "If we can be of any assistance in the future, please contact us"?

If you fell prey to any of the preceding pitfalls, remember that it is sometimes difficult to be tactful and considerate while saying no. Here are some suggestions that beginners have found helpful in sincerely communicating their consideration for their readers. These suggestions should be applied only in situations where the reader and the writer are not personally acquainted. Once writers have polished their craft, they seldom need step-by-step suggestions such as these:

1. Begin with a neutral or positive beginning, such as "The *Hi-Lite* staff should be commended for developing ingenious ideas to raise money to finance their outstanding school newspaper."

2. Develop the reasons for not granting the request before actually refusing it, so that the refusal can be more easily accepted. For example, "Last year, Towers Department Store received more than 100 requests for use of their display windows by charities, high schools, colleges, church groups, and civic organizations. Which of the requests were to have priority? When would we be able to display our own store merchandise? These were some of the problems with which we were faced."

3. Refuse in the most positive manner possible, such as "For this reason, the management of the Towers Department Store has decided that display windows will be used to display store merchandise only, so that customers can always depend on Towers to display the latest in fashions."

4. Include an alternative, if possible. For example, "Because we enjoy reading your high-caliber school newspaper as much as the students do, may I suggest that you have your business manager call me at 555-6251 to discuss advertising space in your next issue. You can depend on us to advertise only things of student interest."

5. End on a pleasant note, such as "Best wishes for another good newspaper publishing year. Perhaps you may want to talk to some of my business associates about advertising in the *Hi-Lite*."

Saying Thank You.   All of us realize the importance of saying thank you in oral communications; it is no less important in written communications. When you have received a helpful reply to your letter of request, you are correct in writing a letter of appreciation to thank your correspondent. If you are ever in doubt about whether to write a letter of thanks, write it. What can you lose? Simply say "Thank you," and don't preface it with "*I want to* thank you." *Thank you* is the most "you" attitude phrase you can use. Why preface it with *I want to* and weaken the forcefulness of the statement?

Ending a letter with the trite and stereotyped "Thanks again" also weakens the effectiveness of the letter. It is redundant, since you have already stated this in your first sentence. If you can honestly and sincerely state how the reply has helped you, do so and end your letter.

Consider the following thank-you letter to Ms. Elizabeth Rathmill, who gave a magnificent keynote presentation on motivation at the Mid-Continent Guidance Counselors' Meeting at Southwest College in St. Joseph, Missouri, on September 21.

Dear Ms. Rathmill:

   Your keynote talk, "How to Motivate Students," set just the right mood for the Mid-Continent Guidance Counselors' Meeting. You will be pleased to know that counselors from throughout the United States are feeling better about themselves and their work because of your sincere, enthusiastic message. Several participants have written to tell me that you were the best speaker that they had ever heard, and I have enclosed copies of their letters for you to read.

   You must know from your long-standing good public speaking experience that a keynote address can either make or break a conference. Evaluations of this conference indicate that it was the best conference ever. That should be proof to you that your presentation was a big success.

                                   Cordially,

Note that the letter is courteous, sincere, and genuine in showing appreciation of Ms. Rathmill's talk. The writer has real proof that the audience was pleased with the speaker's remarks. And how wise of the writer to share the compliments made by members of the audience! Think how pleased the speaker will feel knowing that the comments were genuinely made, because the people writing them had no other motive than to express their sincere reactions.

WRITING ASSIGNMENT

1. You sent an honorarium of $200 to Ms. Elizabeth Rathmill for the speech she made at the Mid-Continent Guidance Counselors' Meeting entitled "How to Motivate Students." She returns it to you, explaining that her agency prevents her from accepting fees. She thanks you for your hospitality and tells you to donate the check to a worthy school-sponsored function. Write the introductory paragraph telling her that the Mid-Continent Guidance Counselors' Association will use the money for a needy student scholarship fund.

_____

_____

_____

_____

_____

_____

_____

_____

_____

_____

_____

_____

_____

_____

2. Your two nephews, Tom and Marc, are avid fans of the Minnesota Twins; so you wrote to Carl Johanson, promotion manager for the Twins, asking for two autographed team pictures for your nephews. You received a prompt reply, and your nephews were delighted with the pictures. Write an appropriate letter of thanks to Mr. Johanson.

_____

_____

_____

_____

_____

_____

_____

_____

_____

_____

_____

unit 9
EXPRESSING GOOD WISHES AND GOODWILL

"It is critical for a service-oriented business like a travel agency to constantly work at building goodwill."

Maria mulled this statement over in her mind and thought: "Just what is goodwill? I know it concerns my customers' good feelings toward me and my business. I think I'm really beginning to appreciate the need for considering things from the reader's point of view! If I can generate sincere interest in my customers and treat them fairly and courteously, I think I will have the key to building goodwill for my agency and to understanding the reader's point of view."

Every business letter should promote good feelings. But if a letter's *primary* purpose is just to be nice or to express good wishes, the letter is then called a *goodwill letter*.

Goodwill messages include announcements and invitations and letters of sympathy, appreciation, congratulations, or praise. Goodwill letters are personal, completely reader-oriented business communications. Because they require a very personal approach, composing these letters calls for a wide range of flexibility by the writer.

Goodwill letters may be written on company stationery or on plain paper, depending upon the situation. Letterhead stationery, however, is not suitable for very personal letters because it takes away from the personal writer-reader relationship and from the individuality of the situation.

EXPRESSING APPRECIATION FOR FAVORS

One of the personal business letters you will write is the "special thanks" letter—a letter to show appreciation for something special that has been done for you. Regardless of whether you think your reader expects some expression of appreciation or not, you should never neglect this opportunity to be nice.

Time is especially important in writing a "special thanks" letter. Promptness usually indicates sincere appreciation.

Some letters of appreciation or special thanks may have greater impact at certain times of the year. For example, special thanks to prompt-paying customers may be sent right after the New Year.

WRITING ASSIGNMENT

Let's see if you can write a "special thanks" letter. Write a letter to your high school coach showing appreciation for a letter of recommendation written on your behalf.

_____

_____

_____

_____

_____

(Continued on page 96.)

_____

_____

_____

_____

_____

_____

Did you remember to do one of the following:

1. Lead off with the main message and tell your reader exactly why you were expressing thanks?
2. Lead up to a thank-you message by arousing your reader's interest with an attention getter before covering all the facts?

Either of these openings could have been used to show appreciation, provided that you unified the entire message by relating everything to appreciation.

Did you remember to:

1. Discuss any pertinent facts or observations?
2. Follow up with an indication that you will return the favor in the future, tell others, or remember the deed for a long time to come?

A follow-up letter of appreciation will bring back to your reader the pleasant, good feeling of being appreciated. When you write a follow-up letter, avoid trite, stereotyped expressions such as "Your service is greatly appreciated." Cold, pompous affirmations of appreciation are worthless.

Now that you've had a chance to analyze your attempt at writing a thank-you letter, you should have no trouble writing a letter for the following exercise.

WRITING ASSIGNMENT

As a result of your persuasive letters, three prominent business executives served as consultants to an advisory council on hiring handicapped workers. With their help, the Hire the Handicapped program has been highly successful in your community. Write a thank-you letter to one of these business executives.

_____

_____

_____

_____

_____

_____

_____

_____

_____

_____

_____

_____

_____

| **CONGRAT-ULATING A SUPERIOR** | Letters of congratulations show thoughtfulness and good manners and are also considered goodwill letters. These letters should be written: |

1. *Promptly* (preferably the same day that the news is received).
2. *Enthusiastically* (perhaps the beginning should be exclamatory).
3. *Informally,* with a conversational style in the body of the letter and also in the salutation and complimentary closing (use first-name basis in the salutation, and avoid *yours* in the complimentary closing).
4. *Sincerely* (show sincere interest in the reader; avoid using *good luck,* which may indicate to the reader that luck accomplished the feat).

The personnel director for Harcourt, Inc., was the chairwoman for a three-day seminar on human relations and communications for managers. David Foster, manager of the accounting department, felt the seminar was a big success and wrote to Bette Hedin telling her so. Consider his letter of congratulation on page 98.

The seminar you chaired, "Human Relations and Communications for Managers," was the best I have ever attended, and I wanted you to know that I thoroughly enjoyed it. Congratulations and thank you!

There were many good sessions, but the one I enjoyed the most was the one conducted by Freddie Winger. I have already put to use some of his ideas on how to deal with professional insult and how to ignore personal condemnation.

All the speakers were excellent, but I single out Mr. Winger because he really hit home for me. Conferences like this one make everyone who participated look forward to more of these personal-growth seminars.

Let's analyze this letter:

1. The tone of the message seems appropriate to the situation in view of the relationship between the writer and the reader.
2. It has a sincere, warm quality. There are no fawning or flattering statements directed to the reader; therefore, the writer cannot be accused of apple-polishing.
3. Even though the writer will probably also congratulate Bette Hedin in person, the letter makes it possible for the reader to share her success with others.
4. The writer gives specific details proving that he isn't writing a "canned" message.

WRITING ASSIGNMENT

Analyze the following letter and be prepared to discuss its strong and weak points.

Another milestone has been passed in your development of the best youth organization in the state of California.

It is unreasonable to expect that my appreciation for your excellent and untiring job can be expressed by the mere writing of words on a sheet of paper. Satisfaction and appreciation for your accomplishments can only be in terms of the contribution to the development of the fine youth involved in the vocational clubs in our state.

It is to this end that I would express not only my own appreciation but the thanks of all the youth whom you have inspired and provided leadership to during the Leadership Conference. May you have the same good luck next year!

EXPRESSING CONGRAT- ULATIONS TO AN EMPLOYEE
It is common practice in business to acknowledge a fifth, tenth, or fifteenth anniversary of a worker. The formality or informality of the letter depends upon the relationship of the employer and the employee. In both informal and formal messages of congratulations, the emphasis is upon the employee's contributions to the company.

WRITING ASSIGNMENT

1. Write a letter of congratulations and good wishes from your employer, the marketing director for Mainline Travel Company, to the production manager, David Phillips, for his tenth year of service to the company. Make up the necessary details.

_____

_____

_____

_____

_____

_____

_____

_____

_____

_____

_____

_____

_____

_____

MAKING ANNOUNCE-MENTS

Announcements that tell your friends and business associates about something that has happened or is going to happen are also goodwill letters. Such personal business messages may be brief; sometimes a single sentence suffices, such as "The Advisory Council of the Washington Business and Office Association will meet at the Seattle Civic Center at 7:30 p.m. on Monday, January 26, to discuss community survey plans."

For a lengthy announcement, you may wish to make the announcement, follow with a discussion of reasons, and then end with suggested action. Remember that the actual announcement is the major purpose of the message. The following announcement is an example of a message from a newly elected executive director.

> **Thank you for the opportunity to act as Executive Director for the Illinois Chapter of the Distributive Clubs of America. Before the year is over, I hope to meet every member individually. All of us have a common goal—preparing youth for the distributive occupations.**
>
> **I am enthusiastic about this new position and eager to get the activities going for this year. With your help, we can make this the DCA's best year in Illinois.**
>
> **As your Executive Director, I plan to give this job all my attention and effort. However, it will be you and your ideas and suggestions that will be the indicators of our future success. Let's rally for a successful year!**

WRITING ASSIGNMENT

Consider the following announcement; then in the space provided, attempt to improve it.

> **We have just recently sold our business to the Federal Bank of Dallas, Texas. Federal Bank will in the near future be serving you, and needless to say we have told them about our many customers who have been the pulse of our business. They are eager to meet you.**

We thank you for the many years that you have banked with us, and we regret that we will no longer be serving you. Thanks for everything and also for the interest you have shown us in the past.

Some of you have been customers for many, many years, and we appreciate your confidence very much. Yes, indeed, it is sad to leave a roster of 25,000 customers.

EXPRESSING SYMPATHY

The most difficult goodwill letters to write are those expressing sympathy for someone who has experienced a personal loss. In writing a condolence, you should try to bring some comfort to the reader and let him or her know that you are sincerely interested. Although the printed card or message is a popular way of conveying this expression of sympathy, a well-written message sometimes adds a personal touch.

Condolences require careful and serious thought. Letters of condolence should be written:

1. *Promptly* (preferably on the same day you receive the news).
2. *Simply* (refer to the event that has occurred; then follow with an expression of sympathy).
3. *Sincerely* (use a serious tone; and offer to be of assistance when it is appropriate).

Consider the following letters:

Dear Mr. Harrigan:

All of us here at General Electronics are grieved by the news of the death of your president, Jean Rousseau. Please accept our most sincere sympathy.

Mrs. Rousseau was a true leader and served as an example to all of us in the community. Her charitable work with the March of Dimes will long be remembered.

Yes, indeed, the memory of Jean Rousseau will continue to serve as an inspiration to the members of the community of Green Plains.

Sincerely,

Dear Tom:

Your co-workers at Daffin Corporation were sorry to learn of your wife's illness. Please accept the flowers we have sent as sincere wishes that she will make both a fast and a complete recovery.

All of us mean it when we say to her, "Get well."

Sincerely,

Both letters are simple and short, and both express sincere sympathy. Although the first letter reminisces a little bit, it doesn't dwell on the sorrow; it is perfectly acceptable.

WRITING ASSIGNMENT

1. You have just learned of the tragic death of Dr. Willa Crawford, one of your former teachers, as a result of a car accident. Dr. Crawford was one of your favorite teachers because she always seemed to have enough time to meet with you to discuss both personal and school problems. In fact, she was also the adviser of the yearbook, and the two of you worked closely together on this project. You think it would be appropriate at this time to write a letter to Dr. Crawford's husband, whom you

have met through the yearbook staff meetings held at the Crawford home.

_____

_____

_____

_____

_____

_____

_____

_____

_____

_____

2. The rising Minnesota River has forced families in the Savage, Minnesota, area to vacate their homes until the waters subside. The governor of Minnesota has asked the federal government for funds for this disaster area. Write an open letter of sympathy to Chadwick Sommers, mayor of Savage, for your employer, who is an adviser for the Future Farmers of America in the adjacent community of Chanhassen. Offer the services of his youth group to help with sandbagging.

_____

_____

_____

_____

_____

_____

_____

_____

unit 10
SELLING AND PROMOTING BY MAIL

Special charters are a big part of the wholesale travel business, and World Wide Tours enjoys the reputation of being one of the biggest wholesalers in the United States. The people in the industry say that Anne Jacobs is responsible for gaining this reputation for World Wide Tours. On several occasions during the seminar sessions, public recognition was given to World Wide Tours' success. Maria enjoyed hearing all the compliments, such as: "Maria, you're lucky to be part of a team headed by Anne Jacobs. If you ever decide to quit your job, let me know." Well, who wouldn't be proud to work for an organization that was nationally known and respected?

As the days passed, and as Maria learned more about succeeding in business through communications, she recognized that her chief executive, Anne Jacobs, was indeed the real reason behind World Wide Tours' success. Take, for example, the case that Hazel Rennard made for the need to write good sales and promotion letters. Most of the suggestions Hazel made were already in practice at World Wide. For three years in a row, the ATAA's award for the best promotion letter had been awarded to Jeffrey McWaters, head of the Advertising and Promotion Department at WWT.

Yes, indeed, like many other successful businesses, World Wide Tours recognizes that every business letter attempts to sell or to promote a product or service. In fact, some people say, "Every business letter is a promotion letter." However, for our discussions, sales and promotion letters will mean only those letters *specifically* intended to sell the products or services of a company.

In large companies (like World Wide Tours), sales and promotion letters are written by specialized personnel in advertising and promotion. Because sales and promotion letters are costly, there are times when even experienced promotion personnel call upon professional advertising agencies and direct-mail specialists to help in writing these letters.

SET THE STAGE

Deciding how to slant your appeal in a sales or promotion letter will involve careful research. Getting ready will mean that you will become fully aware of *what* and *to whom* you are trying to sell or promote. This is necessary if you are to have any success in marketing your product or service.

What you are trying to sell must be conveyed to the reader in descriptive terms, such as size, shape, color, and other physical qualities. It stands to reason it will be for you to direct your appeal. The description you give will allow your reader to form a mental picture of your product or service. Yes, the description is very important; however, the functional use of the product or service will be even more important. But one should supplement the other.

Where will you go to find information about *what* you are trying to sell? Here are some sources:

1. The product itself—physical characteristics, unique features, durability.
2. The resource materials that go into the product—variety used

("ebony wood," "stainless steel," and so on), source of supply ("imported African mahogany," for example).

3. The manner in which it is produced—special equipment used ("deep-oven baked"), skills required ("handcrafted leather"), sanitary measures ("sterile gauze").

Where will you go to find out *who* will buy your product or service? Most often you will attempt to buy or rent lists of names of prospective customers with common interests. You might use lists of college graduates, high school graduates, magazine subscribers, teachers, and so on. Once you have selected the mailing list, you will have to know the following things about your prospective customers:

1. Is the customer a retail buyer or a wholesaler jobber (one who sells to others)?
2. What is the customer's background?
3. What are the customer's needs?
4. What are the customer's likes and dislikes?

Although in direct-mail advertising or selling the same letter is sent to all the prospective customers on the mailing list, every letter has to sound as though it were written especially for each reader. For this reason, research of the prospective customer is of great importance.

HAVE A PLAN	Once you get the facts, your next step is to develop a plan—a plan that will include everything that is necessary to put you on the right path to developing a powerful, polished sales message. Remember, this plan should meet all the requirements of a good request letter and should include all the specifics that are necessary to the particular situation. As a beginning writer, you may wish to use the following three-step plan. It could produce results for you.

1. Get the reader's interest.
2. Describe and explain the product or service so that the customer will want to buy and use it.
3. Make it easy for the reader to act.

Get the Reader's Interest. The money and time spent on the direct-mail campaign will be wasted unless the message is read. Your strategy should start, therefore, with the envelope itself. You may want to consider the following ideas that have been used to entice the prospective customer to open the letter and read it.

1. Make your correspondence resemble first-class mail (it will probably be third-class mail) by using precanceled stamps, imitation stamps, or metered mail.
2. Avoid using a return address so that your customer will be curious to open the letter.
3. Use a window envelope with the prospect's name showing to give the impression that the enclosed material is important.
4. Address the envelope in longhand to reduce the suggestion of mass mailings.
5. Print or type on the envelope an attention-getting statement, such as "Invitation Enclosed" or "Free Gift Offer."

In the past, mass mailings were difficult to camouflage, and many prospective customers recognized the techniques suggested above. In these cases, the costly direct-sales promotion mail campaign never achieved its sales goals, because many readers tossed the envelope into the wastebasket before reading the message.

Within the last ten years, however, people in business have observed the overwhelming popularity of word processing equipment in transforming ideas to printed form. Maria, as you remember, was recently promoted to Senior Correspondent of the World Wide Tours Word Processing Department. Maria uses the latest equipment—a magnetic keyboard with a text-editing display system and a high-speed copy machine. The efficiency of the system allows her to produce many, many individually typed letters at exceptionally high speeds and at a low unit cost. All her letters, even form letters, are individually typed. Therefore, the usual problem of making each form letter in a mass mailing look like an individually typed letter isn't a problem for Maria. For word processing equipment operators, adding inside addresses, personal salutations, and date lines is a simple operation; therefore, every letter can be easily personalized.

With or without the use of specialized typewriters and word processing equipment, the sales and promotion letters must arouse the curiosity of your reader so that he or she will be interested enough to read the beginning of your message. Anytime you can make a reader ask "What is this?" you have accomplished this objective, because the only way the reader can find out is to read on. The following attention getters have been used successfully to get readers interested.

1. An exciting, special offer: "A FREE ONE-WEEK TRIP TO ACAPULCO."
2. A headline in bold type or in a bright color, such as "FREE TO YOU . . ."
3. An illustration, such as a cartoon or a clever drawing.
4. A gadget, such as a shiny new penny, a check, a stamp, or a swatch of cloth.

It is wise to remember that whatever you use as your attention getter should be positive, in good taste, and believable. The purpose of the attention getter is to make the reader ask, "What is this letter all about?"

Hold the Reader's Interest. The best way to prepare a strong sales message that will stimulate the reader's interest is to appeal to basic wants, because *basic wants* are (1) quickly aroused, (2) vigorous and strong, and (3) practically universal. Here is a list of basic wants and the activators or *drives* that make people go after these wants:

BASIC WANTS	DRIVES
Food, drink, and shelter	Enjoyment of appetizing, satisfying food and drink and of a home or apartment
Comfort	Comfortable clothes, furnishings, and surroundings
Security—freedom from fear and danger	Elimination of fearful, painful, dangerous things
Superiority over others	Victory in every race—keeping up with the Joneses
Attraction to the opposite sex	Companionship, love, and affection of the opposite sex
Social approval	Acceptance by friends and associates
Welfare of loved ones	Provision for the welfare of loved ones
Longer life	Enjoyment of life—the possibility of living longer

There are wants other than basic wants. These wants are considered *secondary wants* and are learned or acquired. They develop as we grow older and become more experienced and conscious of our position in society. For selling some products and services, appeals to these secondary wants can be very effective. Secondary wants are not, however, stimulated as quickly as basic wants. A list of secondary wants is shown below, along with examples of sentences that can stimulate them.

SECONDARY WANTS	EXAMPLES
Bargains	**"Make $1 do the work of $4."**
Information	**"Comparison proves the new Cold Air is a great refrigerator to buy. Look at these features."**
Cleanliness	**"Before and after—see what a difference Tinsley Shampoo makes?"**
Efficiency	**"New Smooth Oil starts easier! Makes your engine run cleaner, perform better, last longer."**
Convenience	**"A new instant coffee that tastes as good as your favorite ground coffee!"**
Dependability, quality	**"You can always count on a Wilson Job-Rated Truck!"**
Economy, profit	**"Buy the economy size and save!" And "These tires give 33% more wear."**
Curiosity	**"Don't read this advertisement unless . . ."**

The appeal you choose will depend upon the results of your study of both your product or service and your prospective customers. Once you have chosen the appeal you will use, you will be able to develop your plan for a successful, strong sales message.

As you have seen, a successful sales letter must get attention and hold the reader's interest. However, something more is needed if you expect the spark to catch fire. You must *satisfy* the interest you have aroused. You must provide a bridge, a realistic connection, or you will offend your reader's intelligence.

Consider the following example written by Rita Cole, a participant of the ATAA seminar from Lewiston, Maine.

YOUR SEE-THE-WORLD TRAVEL AGENCY
wants to treat you to ONE WEEK'S STAY on the
beautiful island of MAUI in February for only
$250 round trip!

As a member of the See-the-World Maui Charter Family, you can afford to leave cold, icy, snowy Maine behind for the warmer Hawaiian island of MAUI.

The average daily February temperature in Maui is 75 degrees, making it one of the most compatible February vacation spots in the world. Maui is a sun lover's haven. Its expansive, uncrowded beaches are known world wide for their powder-fine white sand overlooking aquamarine waters. For the more adventurous vacationer, exciting sight-seeing tours and deep-sea diving and fishing are available. The enclosed, full-color brochure gives you an authentic, vivid picture of the treasures of beautiful Maui.

Air Hawaii has really outdone itself on this charter rate. In almost ten years in the travel business, we have never before been able to offer charters to any of the Hawaiian Islands for such a low price.

In order that we may pass this special Maui fare price directly to you, we urge you to call us or write today reserving passage to a week of February heaven. Don't delay and miss this once-in-a-lifetime bargain!

This message is positive and in good taste. It uses an attention getter that sparks interest and is pertinent to what the writer is trying to sell. In the second paragraph the writer satisfies the interest that was originally aroused.

Avoid attention getters that have no relation to the subject of the letter, such as the following:

1. Completely unrelated openings—"Beware! Vicious dog! We don't know if you have a dog or not, but we are willing to de-

liver 26 baby spruce pine trees right to your door for the exceptionally low price of $1.50 each."

2. Negative statements—"Are door-to-door sales representatives plaguing you? If so, you will appreciate our selling Handi-Pak hairbrushes by mail."

3. Remarks insulting to a person's intelligence—"Have you heard that the early bird catches the worm?"

4. Lecture-sermon types of openings—"As a taxpayer, you should be vitally concerned with the expenditures of your city officials."

5. Kidding kinds of openings—"Now you don't want to see me out of a job, do you? Well, if I can't sell you a new Speedy Vacuum, I may be out of a job."

WRITING ASSIGNMENT

Draft an attention-getting, interesting opening for a letter to the business executives in your community encouraging them to purchase advertising space in your school yearbook. All space is one size only—2 by 2 inches—at a cost of $50.

_____

_____

_____

_____

_____

_____

_____

_____

_____

_____

_____

_____ **Describe and Explain.** Another principle to consider in planning an effective sales message is to describe and explain the product or service. You will, of course, have to cover its physical characteristics. To understand the value of your product or service, your reader must have a vivid mental picture of it. Your reader will not be able to appreciate the explanatory message that follows your description unless you have successfully conveyed this picture.

Remember, this description and the explanatory message will be the significant factors that will stimulate the reader to purchase the product or service. The description will have to tell what your product or service will do for the reader by suggesting that one or more of the reader's wants will be satisfied. In other words, a sales letter should carry the same reader-oriented message of all request letters.

Do not try to bluff your reader! Just as the hard sell of the insincere sales representative is quickly recognized, the hard sell of the insincere message, too, is easily detected. Your product or service has to live up to your promises. A deliberate effort on your part to substantiate your claims will register positively with your reader. Many devices have been used successfully, such as:

1. Laboratory tests
2. Testimonials
3. Endorsements
4. Free samples
5. Trial periods
6. Money-back guarantees

WRITING ASSIGNMENT

From the opening that you developed in the previous exercise, write a follow-up description that will explain the benefits of buying advertising space in your yearbook.

_____

_____

_____

_____

_____

_____

_____

_____

_____

_____

_____

_____

_____

_____ **Make It Easy for the Reader to Act.** An effective sales message must also motivate prompt, easy-to-take action. You must give your reader a reason to act at once, because the highest point of interest is when the letter is still in your reader's hands. You will probably have to induce the reader to take prompt action with special discounts, trial periods, free samples, and so on. All these things may be ineffective, however, unless they are offered "for a limited time only." The reader who does not act immediately will probably never act.

To help motivate your reader to prompt action, you may also offer payment plans, delayed billing, or other such helpful measures. Addressed, stamped envelopes are effective, as are convenient order forms. The easier you make it for the reader to answer, the more eager he or she will be to do so. If you expect a reader to answer by telephone, make sure the telephone number is obvious and that extension numbers are given for departments. If a personal visit is necessary, it is important to describe the location and to indicate the store hours, parking facilities, public transportation, and so on.

Consider the sales appeal in the following letter:

Dear Friend:

   The Fund for the Improvement of the Environment needs your help to "Keep America Beautiful." In the past, we have distributed free litter bags to emphasize the need to free our environment from litter. By using them you help remind our community that FIE is devoted to making America a cleaner place in which to live.

   Now we must reevaluate our total budget because of the public demand for us to expand our community services.

For this reason, we must discontinue the FIE tradition of distributing litter bags without charge.

Will you help us continue this worthwhile service by buying your litter bags and distributing them to your customers? You can buy them for as little as $4.70 for 100 bags.

Check the number you will need on the enclosed stamped business reply card, and return it to us today. Your support will help FIE to "Keep America Beautiful."

Sincerely,

The writer does a nice job in this fund-raising letter, which differs slightly from a sales letter in that it does not promise the prospects a product or service. It asks them to support a cause. Appeals such as fund-raising letters cannot offer readers the explanation, description, and prompt action of sales letters. In fact, these tactics would be in poor taste for such letters. This writer presents the message in a dignified manner and attempts to instill in the reader a feeling of wanting to get on the bandwagon and make a contribution.

WRITING ASSIGNMENT

1. Wind up your letter selling advertising space in your yearbook to the business executives in your community. Be sure to motivate them to act!

_____

_____

_____

_____

_____

_____

_____

_____

_____

_____

_____

_____

_____

2. Assume you work at the Breezy Cape Lodge on Willow Lake outside Brainerd, Minnesota, as a secretary for the sales and promotion manager. The editor of the magazine _The Great Outdoors_ has just sent your boss a list of names of fishing enthusiasts residing in the Minnesota area. These prospects are prominent professional business executives. It is now April 20, and your boss wants you to try out your newly acquired sales-letter-writing skills by writing a letter urging these outdoor lovers spend their vacations at your lodge. Since your resort is so popular, for the past two years you have had waiting lists; therefore, reservations should be made by May 10. Some of the facts you might include in your letter are:

a. You have excellent bass and northern pike fishing.
b. You operate a charter plane service from Minneapolis to Willow Lake.
c. You require a $100 deposit for every reservation.
d. You have other facilities, such as boats, cabins, beaches, a nine-hole golf course, and a nightclub for dancing.

Perhaps your sales letter should put particular emphasis on emotional appeals and descriptions. Obviously, the pleasure, satisfaction, and relaxation that a vacationer at your lodge can enjoy will be appealing to today's busy executive.

Use the following space to write your sales-appeal letter. Describe any nonverbal techniques that you use.

_____

_____

_____

_____

_____

_____

(Continued on page 116.)

_____

_____

_____

_____

_____

_____

_____

   Well, how many reservations do you think you'll get? Analyze your answers to the following questions and then make your prediction.

1. Did you attract attention and stimulate interest in your opening message through words and eye appeal (color, layout, and so on)?
2. Did you attempt to study the product and your prospective customers so that you could match your lodge facilities with their vacation needs?
3. Did you use good grammar, correct spelling, logical paragraph development, and so on, to ensure accuracy in expressing your message in your reader's language?
4. Did you talk about the lodge in an honest and believable way, and did you show *proof* of your claims?
5. Did you lead logically, using emotional appeals, to your central theme—vacationing at the Breezy Cape Lodge?
6. Did you include a specific request (preferably a positive statement or command) with a final date for registering for lodge accommodations?
7. Did you make it easy for your customers to reply to your request for early reservations?
8. Did you include a descriptive brochure illustrating the lodge facilities, and did you remember to mention it in your letter? Were the facts in the brochure and in the letter consistent?

   If, in your final analysis, you can answer "yes" to the preceding questions, you will undoubtedly get more than your quota of lodge reservations!

unit 11
ASKING FOR CREDIT

At this morning's session Hazel Rennard, recognizing the importance of adequate cash flow in the travel business, gave special emphasis to the need for healthy accounts receivable. She had heard of too many travel agents who failed because they were careless in granting credit to poor-paying risks.

She introduced the topic by saying: "Travel agencies sell vacations on credit, cemetery directors sell burial plots on credit, banks sell 'instant cash' on credit. It is safe to say that the country is a credit card society. A 'buy now, pay later' or 'use the other guy's money' philosophy makes credit big business in the United States."

Let's take advantage of some of the background information Hazel gave the group before we learn to write credit communications.

PERSONAL CREDIT

Personal credit is credit that a business or a bank grants to an individual customer, such as you. The credit card is very popular for personal or retail credit and serves as an identification at the time of purchase. The latest type of charge card is the bank credit card, such as Visa and Master Card. Merchants who honor such cards can receive an immediate payment from the bank, which acts as the clearinghouse for credit charges and collections. This type of charge card is very popular because it allows the small merchant the advantage of offering credit to many customers and it allows the customers with no cash to buy goods from many merchants merely on the strength of the credit card.

There are several different arrangements that can be made for personal credit. Two popular kinds of accounts are the regular charge and the revolving credit plans.

The *regular charge account* permits the customer to use an identification plate to purchase items. Usually the customer receives a statement at the end of each month, and the amount is payable on receipt of the statement. Some companies, however, use cycle billing for regular charge accounts to ensure a continous flow of money into the firm. Billing, in other words, is done on certain days each month according to alphabetic sequence of last names. The regular charge account allows the customer the greatest credit freedom.

Revolving credit is the same as the regular charge account with one basic difference. The entire bill does not have to be paid upon receipt of the statement. If the bill is not fully paid, a carrying charge is added to the balance on the next statement. This charge may appear to be a disadvantage; however, the customer can enjoy the benefit of charging as much as he or she wishes and making only small payments.

Customers make formal application before credit is issued. In most instances, the customer fills out a form. The firm checks the customer's credit rating by consulting a commercial credit book and by checking the references listed on the customer's application form before granting credit.

WRITING ASSIGNMENT

You have been purchasing many goods and services from the Deephaven Variety Store during the past six months and are pleased with their merchandise and service. Write to them, requesting a credit application form. Tell them you are also interested in receiving information about both their regular charge and their revolving credit plans.

_____
_____
_____
_____
_____
_____
_____
_____
_____
_____
_____

BUSINESS CREDIT

Just as businesses extend personal credit to individuals, businesses also extend credit to other businesses. Shipping firms, manufacturers, wholesalers—all extend credit to retail businesses.

Unlike personal credit, no credit cards are used for business credit. However, businesses also fill out application forms when applying for credit from other businesses. Sometimes, businesses may apply for credit through a letter accompanied by financial statements. Generally, credit is requested up to a specified amount. Under the terms of most credit agreements, the buyer agrees to pay the full amount of each monthly invoice within a specified time, usually 30 days. Here is a letter requesting credit from an art supply dealer:

Dear Mr. Hernandez:

In January of last year, I opened the Deephaven Craft Shoppe on Highway 101 in Waverly. Since then, I have been purchasing merchandise c.o.d. from you. With your approval, I would like to establish a credit line of $1,000 with the customary terms of 2/10, n/30.

In the past ten months, my store's monthly gross income averaged $5,000. Upon purchase, I secured a $5,000 loan from Federal Savings and Loan on Main Street. The monthly payment on this loan is $200; the current balance is approximately $1,800. The rent for the store is $500 each month. There are no other loans or monthly obligations.

Two years ago, my husband and I purchased the one-family home at 17 Finney Road, where we now live. To buy this home, we secured a $30,000 mortgage from Westerleigh Savings and added our down payment of $15,000 to meet the purchase price. The total monthly payment for both the mortgage plus tax is $315. We have no other outstanding debts.

The following people have given me permission to use their names as references: Mr. John Aliano, Vice President, Coleman and Matzka Public Relations, Inc.; and Dr. Laura Hanks, St. Matthew's Hospital. Both are here in Waverly.

Enclosed is our latest financial statement. If you need any other information, please do not hesitate to let me know.

                                    Sincerely,

In this letter, the writer gives a brief financial account of the business and also her financial statement. This information will certainly help the wholesaler make a decision. She asks for a specific maximum credit line of $1,000 and for standard terms—2/10, n/30—which means that (1) the buyer may deduct a 2 percent discount from the net amount if she pays within 10 days and (2) the net amount is due within 30 days.

Without these credit terms, the wholesaler would have to make the trucker responsible for collecting for each delivery to the Craft Shoppe—and there may be as many as three deliveries a week! Obviously, the wholesaler would prefer sending, and the retail craft store would prefer paying, one monthly bill.

WRITING ASSIGNMENT

Apply for credit with Blunt-Johnson Art Supplies and enclose your order for materials totaling $150. You have owned your own business for six months now and bought all of your merchandise on a c.o.d. basis. Now that you're settled and doing well, you would like to establish a $1,000 credit line. Write a letter to Mr. Alfred Chin, comptroller for Blunt-Johnson. Make your financial statistics as realistic as possible.

_____

_____

_____

_____

_____

_____

_____

_____

_____

_____

_____

_____

_____

_____

GRANTING CREDIT PRIVILEGES

When a credit application or letter has been checked and approved, a personal letter is written to the customer to announce the good news. This letter should be not only a statement of the terms and conditions of the credit agreement but a sales letter as well. It may be compared to a note of welcome, so the reader should be told immediately that credit has been granted. It should say, "Welcome—you're in!"

The opening statement should get the relationship off to a good start by making the reader aware of being "in" as far as your family of customers is concerned. It should reflect warmth and sincerity and should welcome the new credit relationship enthusiastically. Even if it has been difficult to reach a favorable decision, you should avoid any hint of a grudging tone, stiffness, or formality.

Your letter, however, must do more than merely announce the good news. It must also build goodwill and encourage the customer to use the new credit privileges. Consider the following favorable response to a personal credit application:

Dear Mr. Cohen:

All of us at Wilson's are proud because you chose to become a regular charge customer of our store. We are pleased to announce that today you are listed along with almost 650,000 other charge customers and are eligible to begin charging your purchases as of tomorrow, January 10.

It is now our job to make sure that you always maintain a feeling of confidence in us. But it's my job specifically to urge everyone at Wilson's to spread out the "royal carpet" each time you come into our store.

Sincerely,

This message makes Mr. Cohen feel proud to be included as one of the charge customers at Wilson's. Notice also that the writer specifically states the date on which the reader can start charging his purchases.

WRITING ASSIGNMENT

Rewrite the following "Welcome—you're in" letter granting credit privileges to a new business in your town.

Dear Ms. Jeffrey:

After checking your references, we have decided that you are a safe risk.

We certainly hope that you will accept the responsibility that goes along with getting credit—that is, making your payments within 30 days of receipt of our monthly statement. Of course, if you are a shrewd business person, you will take advantage of the 2 percent discount allowed on payments made within 10 days of receipt of our statements.

Since this is a special privilege given only to qualified businesses, we will expect you to adhere closely to all policies regarding your account.

Sincerely,

_____
_____
_____
_____
_____
_____
_____
_____
_____
_____

REFUSING PERSONAL CREDIT

Refusing personal credit is a more difficult situation to handle. When you say "no" to a credit applicant, you are really saying that you doubt the applicant's ability to pay his or her bills. In a way you are doubting the writer's character or moral fiber, a serious charge!

Some writers think it best to come right out and tell applicants why they are being refused credit. However, most good writers agree that the refusal should be more tactful. In either case, the customer should be encouraged to buy on a cash basis. You can see that this will be quite a challenge for any writer whether experienced or inexperienced.

> **Dear Mr. Giegle:**
>
> **Unfortunately, you cannot expect to get credit at our store with your record of poor payment on other charge accounts. We have had too many unfortunate experiences with people such as you, and for this reason we have made it our company policy not to accept applications for credit from poor risks.**
>
> **I'm sure you will understand why we have had to refuse your request. Thank you for applying.**
>
> **Sincerely,**

Obviously, this is a negative response. Even if it is honest, it isn't tactful to state your position in such negative terms. There is no question that this customer will think twice before buying something even on a cash basis at this store after being treated so rudely.

Consider the next solution:

Dear Mr. Giegle:

   Thank you for applying for credit at our store. It is always a compliment to have cash customers request credit. Although we would like to grant you credit, I am afraid we cannot do so at this time.

   Upon checking your references, we were told that you have unpaid balances of several months' standing at two stores. When you pay these accounts, you will be eligible to make application again in six months. We will be very happy to reconsider your application at that time. Until then, we certainly hope that you will take advantage of the many sales that we will be having this summer on a cash basis.

                               Sincerely,

This letter is straightforward and honest, but it is also tactful and courteous. It doesn't mention anything about a lack of trust, and the last paragraph softens the refusal by suggesting an alternative.

WRITING ASSIGNMENT

How would you answer the following letter, which was attached to Mrs. Glenda Kernan's credit application form? Your mail-order house cannot extend credit to her no matter how honest she appears to be.

   I think your catalog is better than ever, and I mean it! Your bargains have saved me money, and your service has saved me time. I would like to apply for your regular charge account privileges.

   Since I was graduated from college last June, I have been working as an editorial assistant for Sports magazine for $200 a week. My husband will be graduated from college

next June. He already has a promise of a job from Aldrick Imports, where he could start in September as a management trainee at a yearly salary of $9,200.

We pay $245.75 a month for our rent. In addition, I pay $180 a month for my student loans. My husband will start repaying his student loans next September when he starts working.

We have only one credit card, the SuperCard. Our present SuperCard balance is about $200.

We have many references as to our character. Having credit privileges at your store would certainly help us a great deal, so please consider my enclosed credit application.

Write your reply below.

_____

_____

_____

_____

_____

_____

_____

_____

_____

_____

_____

Tough one to say "no" to? Sure it was. It's never easy to say "Not now—maybe later," especially when the request appears to be so honest and so necessary. You should have been very tactful when you refused this customer.

1. Did you include a statement of appreciation for the writer's request?

2. Did you honestly explain why you had to refuse the request? Did you do so before you actually refused? Sometimes this softens the actual refusal.
3. Did you make concrete, helpful suggestions as to what action she could take now?
4. Did you encourage her to continue buying on a cash basis?
5. Did you close with the hope-for-the-future attitude? Did you attempt to keep your customer's goodwill?

If you answered "yes" to the above questions, you probably lessened the blow of your refusal to this honest person's request for credit. Also, you probably retained her as a cash-paying customer —a letter-writing skill to be envied.

REFUSING BUSINESS CREDIT

Although letters refusing business credit are also ticklish to write, they are a little less so than those refusing personal credit. In refusing business credit, you don't have to get at such things as moral duty or character. A more straightforward approach may be taken because less-than-desirable financial conditions or poor cash flow situations are common in business. For this reason a more optimistic approach may be taken.

Note how the following refusal of business credit is handled:

Dear Mr. Dickinson:

Thank you for sending us your financial statement and your credit application. You will be happy to know that your credit references spoke highly of you as a beginning businessman.

Your new store is located in one of Morristown's busiest shopping centers and has all the conditions necessary to prosper. However, our records show that two other pizza restaurants have not been successful in your location. Until we have an opportunity to estimate what your potential is in the Mall Square, we must ask you to deal with us on a cash basis.

In order to help you get your restaurant off to a quick success, we are offering you a 5 percent cash discount rather than our customary 2 percent. This savings can be passed on to your customers. By ordering smaller quantities

of restaurant supplies more frequently, you will keep just enough stock on hand to handle your weekly business. Through this cash buying, you will build your business on a sound financial basis that will help you establish lines of credit in the near future.

You may want to take advantage of our May special on one-gallon cans of Progresso Tomato Purée at $9.80 a case. If you call our order desk today, you can have delivery by the end of the next week.

Sincerely,

WRITING ASSIGNMENT

Sharon and Adrien Wilson, owners of the Luggage Library, a retail store specializing in luggage, briefcases, wallets, and other leather goods, have written to your firm for business credit. Specifically, the Wilsons have asked the Hercules Leather Company for a $3,000 credit line with the usual terms of 2/10, n/30.

Although the Wilsons have established good credit in the two years in which they have owned the Luggage Library, Hercules company policy grants a maximum credit line of $500 to new customers (with 2/10, n/30 terms). After a six-month period, a customer can increase the credit line.

Write a letter to the Wilsons refusing their request for a $3,000 credit line.

_____

_____

_____

_____

_____

_____

_____

_____

_____

_____

unit 12
WRITING LETTERS ABOUT PROBLEMS

"Today," said Hazel Rennard, "we'll tackle one of the most important reasons for writing business letters: to solve problems. Every business receives letters from unhappy customers. Travel agencies are no exception. How would you like to answer this one?"

Dear Vacation Spoilers:

Thank you for making my first vacation in ten years a big, flat flop! I want you to know that from the time I arrived at the airport for what your brochure called "a trip to paradise" until I walked off the three-hour-late return flight, I met with nothing but disaster.

What happened to me on my trip is almost macabre. Nothing but nothing puts a vacationer in a better mood than to get up at 3:30 a.m. to make a 5:30 a.m. flight only to stand around for five hours waiting for her "trip to paradise."

I won't spend too much time telling you about the flight out, since the incidents seem almost small now compared to the fiasco I got into in "paradise." However, some passengers, I am sure, would be irate to have a sleepy-eyed, cranky steward spill coffee all over their Sunday-best clothes. But how can you complain when the helpful steward tells you that you can have it cleaned at the airline's expense when you get to "paradise"? And, of course, having to sit as straight as a board for 3½ hours because the seat wouldn't recline allowed the stains to "dry in place." On a more positive note, though, I have to admit I appreciated the dried-out roll that was served for "lunch," because it prevented me from starving to death.

At last, the captain said, "Prepare for landing." I couldn't wait to get out of that dirty, crowded airplane. All I could think of was "paradise at last!" That vision of "paradise" went quickly up in smoke, though, when:

1. The ground transportation arrangements fell through.
2. Because of overbooking, my single-room request was changed to a double.
3. Two of the three sight-seeing trips were canceled.
4. It rained in "paradise" for five of my seven days.
5. There wasn't any hot water after 9:00 each morning.
6. The tour guide disappeared after the first day.
7. The hotel coffee shop was closed for remodeling.
8. The pool was closed for cleaning on one of the two sunny days.

What could be a more exciting ending to a vacation like mine than to get home three hours late only to find that my bags were still in "paradise"! I hope they have a better time than I did.

I am thinking of seeking legal action. Unless you refund my entire tour cost, I'm going to sue you.

"Obviously, the writer, Delores Caufield, is so angry at her travel agency that she can hardly see straight. If all these things happened to her on one trip, she has every right to be in a rage. But, unfortunately, writing a letter blasting someone does little more than allow her to vent her anger. It does *not* help to get results. There are effective ways to ask for adjustments, and there are effective ways to answer adjustment requests. Let's see how."

WRITING LETTERS ASKING FOR ADJUST-MENTS	A first reaction to stupid mistakes is anger. Usually, no matter who is at fault, blunders create stress situations. People exposed to stress experience emotional and physical reactions that affect their minds as well as their bodies. For example, a person's blood pressure may rise excessively during extreme irritation. Depending upon their maturity and their ability to handle these physical changes, some people may explode internally when put in pressure situations. They allow their emotions to control their thinking.

All of us can and must learn to cope with stress; if we do not, our health will certainly suffer. Stress situations must be dealt with head-on. A mind-set must be developed, such as: "I'll only make my point in this letter (or memorandum) if I am even-tempered. By being even-tempered, I can make my point logically and rationally, and I will not run the risk of allowing my emotions to dictate my actions and words." With this mind-set, a person learns to practice self-control of both body and mind. So the first criterion for writing a good letter or memo asking for an adjustment is to control your emotions and think before you write. Avoid anger, sarcasm, accusations, and personal attacks, such as: "People told me not to do business with you. They warned me that you weren't stable enough to run a business!" Such words as "big, flat flop," "disorganized," "disgrace," "rotten service," "worthless," and "no good" are emotion-packed words that show the reader that you are not in control.

When writing letters asking for adjustments, concentrate on the *purpose* of your letter. By doing this, you should be able to (1) give a straightforward explanation of what the problem is by documenting dates, amounts, persons involved, actual descriptions, and other precise information; (2) specify the loss to you; (3) appeal to the reader's sense of fair play for prompt investigation; and when possible, (4) suggest an acceptable adjustment.

By concentrating on your purpose for writing, you can learn to hold your emotions intact! Let's say that you ordered a blue wool blanket from a mail-order firm. When the blanket arrives, you discover that the company has sent you a lime-green blanket. Since you want a blue blanket (the color matches your room), you should write the mail-order house and ask them to exchange the green blanket for a blue one. The purpose of your letter is to get a blue blanket.

In planning to write the letter asking for a blue blanket in exchange for a lime-green one, you should recognize that the letter is basically a request letter. Therefore, keep in mind the writing principles you learned for request letters, making sure that you state a definite request, motivate the reader to reply to your request, and help your reader to meet your request. Remember to:

1. Give an explanation of your problem—"On January 10, I ordered a No. 67421 light blue fleece wool blanket from your Winter Catalog; and on January 22 I received a lime-green wool fleece blanket."
2. Explain the loss to you—"The lime-green blanket clashes with my newly redecorated powder-blue bedroom."
3. Appeal to the reader's sense of pride and fair play—"Certainly you wouldn't want me to keep something I didn't order, would you? Please tell me how I can return the lime-green blanket without cost to me so that you can exchange it for the No. 67421 blue blanket I originally ordered."

WRITING ASSIGNMENT

You have been so successful in writing routine letters that you are now ready to write this unusual "I've got a problem" letter.

A little over ten months ago, your employer purchased an EXACTO desk clock and radio. After two weeks the clock stopped running every six hours or so. Since there is no local service for EXACTO timepieces in your city, you sent the clock back to EXACTO, Inc. Three months and two letters later, you got it back. But within two days, it was back to its old tricks—stopping every six hours or so. Your boss is darn angry and emphatically tells you to write a letter to EXACTO, Inc., asking them for permission to return the clock to the factory again. By the way, this time your boss wants results—not in three months but more like three days! How would you write your letter telling them about your problem? Use the following space to write your letter.

(Continued on page 132.)

_____

_____

_____

_____

_____

_____

_____

_____

_____

1. Did you remember to describe the situation thoroughly and to explain that you paid for a desk clock and radio more than ten months ago but still have not had the opportunity to enjoy it?
2. Did you motivate your reader by appealing to fair play?
3. Did you remember to alert your reader that EXACTO's image was at stake?
4. Did you also alert your reader to the fact that EXACTO's image could be restored by either repairing the desk clock and radio or replacing it?
5. Did you specifically inform your reader as to what action you expected?
6. Did you remember to keep your emotions intact, yet let your reader know you meant business?
7. Did your tone reflect a positive attitude by showing that you believed your reader was eager to remedy the situation and maintain your goodwill?

ANSWERING LETTERS THAT ASK FOR ADJUSTMENTS

Just as you may write letters asking for adjustments, you will also probably have to answer such letters. The requests made in letters will sometimes allow you to say "yes" and will at other times force you to say "no." Your job will be more difficult when you must refuse the adjustment—especially if the writer was antagonistic and belligerent. In any case, you must remain in control and use tact and fairness in dealing with the request.

Letters requesting adjustments demand prompt replies. To the person requesting the adjustment, the problem is the most important thing in the world; so don't frustrate the writer further by delaying your response.

When answering letters that ask for adjustments, concentrate on the following:

1. Include all the qualities of the goodwill letter.
2. Do not insinuate that the person requesting adjustment is an agitator or a troublemaker. Avoid negative terms like "your complaint" (you could say "your letter") or "your unfortunate experience of April 10" (you could say "the April 10 incident").
3. Give reasonable explanations. In a letter granting the adjustment request, include only what is absolutely necessary in the explanation; however, in a letter refusing the adjustment, be sure to explain thoroughly before you turn your reader down.

The letters that make adjustments must also develop a healthy mind-set. The best way to do this is to concentrate on the purpose of your response. Convince the customer, even if he or she is wrong, that you maintain the philosophy that the customer is always important. Welcome the opportunity to give personal attention.

Think of the adjustment letter as a goodwill letter. It is your opportunity to rebuild or strengthen your image. You will know what to say—sometimes it will be "yes" and sometimes it will be "no." It will be up to you to decide how to say it. Your goal should be *to renew a friendship*.

Answering "Yes." The easiest type of adjustment letter you will write is the one that allows you to say "yes" to a customer's claim. However, certain precautions should be taken:

1. Don't dwell upon the problem.
2. Use inoffensive, neutral words in place of offensive negative language.
3. Don't harangue about who is at fault. If it is you, admit it and apologize; if it isn't, just forget it. Say "yes" and end the letter.

The routine "yes" letter should include a statement that tells your reader that you are thinking alike. Remember that to the reader the most important element of this letter is the granting of the request. Thus the "yes" letter usually will not require a lengthy explanation; giving the reader what he or she wants will be enough.

In a more serious situation where the person making the claim is hostile and angry, you should attempt to smooth things out before granting the request: "Thank you for informing us that your Order 26742, dated March 15, arrived two days after your Anniversary Sale. Of course, you may return the merchandise for full credit."

Finally, you should make an attempt to regain the confidence of your customer. It is important that you sound convincing and sincere: "You will want to take advantage of the quantity discounts on White Sale items. These discounts are being offered early in July, with delivery ensured for the August white sales." Don't make impossible promises, such as "We assure you that such a thing will never happen again."

Consider the following letter:

Dear Mr. Edgarton:

No wonder you were confused by our billing for the expenses incurred during your July 12 Regional Sales Meeting held at our hotel. Mistakenly, we charged you for the meeting room that we said would be free.

Please deduct the $30 charge for the meeting room and send us your payment for only $142.50.

Thank you for choosing the Innwood Manor. It was a pleasure to serve you. We certainly hope that you had a successful meeting and that you will come back to the Innwood soon!

Sincerely,

This message is good because the writer admits the error and grants the customer's request for adjustment without overstressing the mistake. Notice that the writer does not promise that this will never happen again, because such a promise would be impossible to keep. The friendly closing ends the message on a positive note.

Answering "No." There are times when it will be impossible for you to say "yes" to a claim. It may be because the article returned is a sale item, the warranty on the appliance has expired, the product has performed as well as can reasonably be expected, or someone else such as the transportation company is at fault. Sometimes it will be necessary to say "no."

No matter how you look at it, this will be bad news to the reader, but you don't have to write a gloomy letter. Instead, use tact and other skills of effective business letter writing to make the best of the situation. In some instances, you may not have to refuse. You may be able to imply the refusal rather than specifically state the refusal. In any case, the refusal, either expressed or implied, should follow a diplomatic explanation.

> **Thank you for taking advantage of the Daisy Sale on January 3-9. For the protection of all our customers, swimsuits must be fitted in our store and are not exchangeable. This store policy conforms to Health Regulation Law 231.**

Before discussing the "no" letter any further, let's see how you would handle the following situation.

WRITING ASSIGNMENT

You are working for a candy manufacturing firm. One of your customers, the Parker Drugstore, ordered 150 boxes of candy in assorted sizes for the Easter season. Slow payment on the part of the Parker Drugstore forced you to write two collection letters. Finally, they sent a check for 100 boxes sold and asked if they could return the other 50 boxes for a credit of $102. Because they have given you their business for the past five years, you are not eager to lose them as a customer. But candy is a perishable item and should always be fresh and stored at room temperature. You cannot possibly do business the way they want you to. You would be encouraging customers to overorder, and you would find yourself in the position of having to accept hard, stale, dry candy. This type of service would be costly and unprofitable. Your boss has just breezed into your office and said: "That Frank Parker must be losing his mind. Why, we would have to double our prices to cover losses if we did it his way. Write to him immediately and refuse the adjustment he requests."

Write your letter on a separate sheet of paper—and don't forget that Frank Parker is a paying customer.

Well, how did you do? Not as easy as saying "Yes, Frank, you may return the 50 boxes of candy," was it? Evaluate your letter using the following criteria:

1. Was your overall attitude diplomatic? In other words, did you turn him down but still make him feel that you did everything possible to help him out?
2. Did you attempt to clear yourself of any blame that Mr. Parker could place on you for refusing to accept the candy?
3. Were you as positive as possible in your attempt to explain your refusal to accept the candy before actually doing so?
4. Did you imply a refusal rather than express it explicitly so as to make the refusal less painful to the customer?
5. Did you attempt to be helpful, such as by suggesting a new sales promotion idea to move the 50 boxes of candy that were not sold?
6. Did you attempt a subtle technique in your implied refusal, such as moving smoothly but rapidly to a new subject? Once again, you might have used the sales promotion idea. This technique can communicate refusal without explicitly expressing it.

Answering "Yes" and "No." Sometimes a reply to a request letter must be a combination of saying "yes" to part of it and "no" to the other part. This letter is slightly more difficult than the letter saying "yes" and slightly less difficult than the letter saying "no." A good rule of thumb is to accent the "yes" part early in the letter and to play down the "no" part of the letter.

WRITING ASSIGNMENT

Hazel Rennard felt that her people were ready to handle a really big writing assignment, so she asked the participants to respond to the "big, flat flop vacation" letter on page 128. Are you ready to handle this assignment? Good! Write to Ms. Delores Caufield to tell her that you cannot refund the entire cost of her vacation. More importantly, though, see if you can convince her that your travel agency is not all "bad news." Use a separate sheet of paper.

unit 13
COLLECTING UNPAID ACCOUNTS

Hazel Rennard just introduced the resource speaker, Mr. William Stock, president of the Palm Springs/Southern California Travel and Tours, who will discuss the topic of collection letters. Let's listen.

"The relationship between granting credit and collecting unpaid accounts should be very close. Well-managed credit policies minimize the number of collection letters that need to be developed as well as the degree of severity of language in the messages themselves. In most organizations, sales departments and credit departments have separate duties and different philosophies, which in some ways are both good and not so good.

"A sales department needs and wants to increase sales. Its primary objective is to please customers so as to increase sales. A credit department needs and wants to keep current on its accounts receivable (money owed by customers). Its primary objective is to collect money and to keep accounts receivable current. Sometimes salespeople want to 'win friends and influence customers' at all costs (by making credit terms available to anyone), while credit people want to avoid unpleasant collection letters at all costs (by making credit terms too strict and by writing offensive letters to collect slightly late accounts).

"A certain amount of pull from either direction of thinking (sales department versus credit department) is healthy for an organization; however, the two departments must maintain a smooth working relationship in order to avoid conflict in company goals. The sales department must sell goods and services, and the credit department must collect accounts. Both must do their jobs or the business will be in trouble."

Maria took detailed notes because she had heard some sales people complain that WWT's credit manager was too strict about granting business credit. Mr. Stock's points regarding the responsibility of credit and collection departments make it clear to Maria why Joe Rocco, the credit manager at World Wide Tours, tends to be more cautious about credit than the sales representatives. Let's see what we can learn about collection letters and how to write them from the information given by Mr. Stock.

The major emphasis here is to develop a series of collection letters to collect unpaid business accounts; these letters differ from those used to collect unpaid individual customer accounts. In the travel business, for example, individual customers pay for their tickets in advance (except for travelers who pay for their airline tickets with credit cards), while business accounts pay for their tickets on a monthly basis using an approved credit line. Although the telephone is sometimes used to collect business accounts (a fairly common practice in the small-loan companies), the written message can be more effective and less humiliating to both the collector and the debtor.

DESIGNING A COLLECTION SERIES

It makes good sense to design collection letters with a dual purpose; namely, to collect debts and maintain goodwill—in other words, get the money and keep the customer. Even though you have the right to seek what is yours because the customer has violated the agreement, your attitude should still be that the customer is always right. You should still cater to the customer's goodwill. Therefore, you must hold anger and disgust in check. Probably the most important thing you can do in opening your letter is to encourage your reader to read it to the end.

Strictly speaking, *collection* suggests a physical act, but you will never actually *collect* money. When you plan a series of pay-up letters, your aim will be to design and organize a series of letters that will *persuade* or *sell* the reader on the idea that it will be advantageous to pay up rapidly. Avoid scolding or sermon-type discussions. They will only further antagonize or bore your reader. You should attempt to develop a program or series of letters based on the trust you had in granting the credit in the first place. Your program should attempt to persuade a delinquent customer to develop better paying habits, but at the same time it should keep the customer happy.

Persuading customers to pay up is, by its very nature, negative and reflects on personal integrity and honor. Therefore, writing collection letters will require careful planning and organization on your part.

Once the credit and collection departments recognize the delinquent accounts, they attempt to make a systematic yet flexible plan for collection. Usually the plan is to send a series of letters that get progressively more forceful. The letters are sent until payment is made. A typical letter series to persuade the customer to pay up will have four stages.

First Stage.   The first stage is the notification stage. Some firms send out second and third statements, which are duplicate copies of the original. Then, if the customer does not respond, the account is declared delinquent. Once the account is considered delinquent, it is time to begin sending the collection series. A printed notice or sticker which informally requests payment may be attached to a statement, or a spearate reminder may be sent. This type of reminder is usually mild and quite impersonal.

Second Stage.   The second stage is a letter sent in place of the impersonal reminder. This letter is usually very mild and attempts to promote goodwill.

Third Stage.   The third stage, the discussion stage, is actually the meat of the collection series. It begins when you no longer believe that the customer *will* pay. The purpose is to convince the reader that he or she *should* pay. Sometimes a series of discussion letters may be sent with each letter stressing one or more appeals designed to persuade the customer to pay up.

Fourth Stage.   The fourth stage follows when the discussion stage has failed. Usually only one letter is written giving the customer a final chance to pay up before any last-resort action will be taken, such as turning the account over to a collection agency or to an attorney.

Let's look at each of the four stages in detail.

FIRST: NOTIFYING THE CUSTOMER

Notifying your customer that his or her account is overdue is the first step in the collection series. At this stage you feel that the customer will pay; therefore, hopefully, the reminders will induce an explanation of why payment has not been made. These are always impersonal appeals; the first one may be a duplicate of the original invoice. This may be followed by a more intense effort, perhaps a statement with a rubber-stamp overdue reminder, such as:

YOUR ACCOUNT
IS PAST DUE

or perhaps an invoice with an overdue-reminder sticker attached, such as:

PROTECT YOUR
CREDIT RATING
PAY NOW

YOUR ACCOUNT IS
___DAYS OVERDUE

Remember, these reminders are used first because you feel that the customer will pay and will do so promptly.

SECOND: THE PAY-UP NOTICE OR LETTER

Naturally, all credit and collection departments hope that the reminders they send out will be successful, that payment will be made promptly. How easy life would be! Unfortunately, there is no question that some customers will not make restitution unless they are prodded to pay up.

Several means of communication can be used effectively. A face-to-face meeting would probably prove the most effective (if it could be arranged). Also, a telephone conversation would be more personal and effective than a letter. Both of these means would be practical only if distance were not a factor.

The letter, however, is the most common means of prodding the customer during the "customer will pay" stage. This letter is sent when impersonal reminders have failed to produce payment. The letter is tactful, courteous, and helpful. It may or may not be a form letter. It may be preprinted or individually typed. Because of the commonplace use of automatic typewriters and magnetic tape typewriters, the trend is toward individually typed letters rather than fill-in form letters. Examples of both follow:

- **Individually Typed Form Letter**

Dear Dr. Svendsen:

This is to remind you that your account, No. 6742, amounting to $564.42, is now three months past due.

If you have already mailed us your check, thank you. If not, use the enclosed stamped envelope to send us your check for $564.42 today.

Sincerely,

- **Fill-In Form Letter**

Dear _____:

This is to inform you that $_____ is now three months past due on your account, No. _____.

Please remember that your credit was granted with the understanding that payment would be made under terms of Net 30 days.

Please mail your check for $_____ in the enclosed stamped, addressed envelope today!

Sincerely,

WRITING ASSIGNMENT

The Harold Klinker Manufacturing Company, 85 Murdock Drive, Raleigh, NC 27607, has been an excellent business account for two years. Now, for the first time, Mr. Klinker is ten days overdue in paying his 30-day account. Write Mr. Klinker to remind him of the $980 overdue account. (Three of the company's engineers flew to Chicago first class for the National Association of Engineers meeting on January 7 to 10.)

_____

_____

_____

_____

_____

_____

_____

_____

_____

THIRD: THE "YOU OUGHT TO PAY" LETTER

Obviously, if you haven't heard from the customer after the reminders and the pay-up letter, you can reasonably conclude that the customer *will not* pay. It is then your responsibility to persuade the customer that he or she *ought* to pay. This stage is actually the challenge of your collection series. You must decide whether to write one "you ought to pay" letter or more than one, and you must design each for a special appeal that will induce your reader to pay up.

It will be necessary to design this letter or these letters to:

1. Arouse interest by doing something unexpected. Don't forget that the customer has received your reminders; therefore, even before opening the envelope your reader will expect an "According to our records" or "Your account is now 3 months past due." Why repeat what has already been ignored? Use a new approach. Open with a statement that will arouse interest as well as motivate a reply.
2. Motivate through carefully chosen appeals. Let such things as customer relationships, amount involved, and previous correspondence with the customer serve as your guide. Frequently used appeals are as follows:

   Fair play. Logical appeal stating how only *you* have carried out the terms of a mutual agreement.

Ego. Emotional appeal showing that self-respect and reputation are at stake and that prompt payment can restore the reader's image.

Sympathy. Emotional appeal telling the debtor that you need the money to keep going. This appeal is usually used when you and your debtor are good friends. It should be used with discretion, because your reader may interpret it to mean that you're in financial difficulty.

Cooperation. Logical appeal inviting the customer to discuss the case with you. This logical appeal may be used to induce the customer to make partial payment by showing that you are open-minded and understanding and willing to cooperate.

Economy. Logical appeal showing the debtor how economy results when prompt payment is made. Prompt payment means lower operating costs, and lower operating costs mean lower prices for the customer.

Fear. Emotional appeal telling the debtor of drastic action that must follow—canceling credit privileges, turning the account over to a collection agency, or repossessing the goods. This appeal can be used when all others have failed.

Although the different appeals have been listed separately, you may wish to use more than one in the "customer ought to pay" letter or letters.

3. Make it clear what you expect the reader to do. If you must have full payment, make it clear. If partial payment will be acceptable, make that clear. Make sure that you restate the amount due and identify the account so the customer will have no opportunity to misinterpret what action you want him or her to take. Since the account is long past due, immediate payment is expected.

4. Help your reader to act easily. Provide physical assistance, such as a stamped, addressed envelope—anything that will serve as another reminder to pay up!

WRITING ASSIGNMENT

1. It is now February 3, and you still have not heard from the Harold Klinker Manufacturing Company. Write one "you ought to pay" letter encouraging Mr. Klinker to clear up his unpaid account. Use a separate sheet of paper.

2. It is now March 10, and Harold Klinker has not made a response to any of your reminders to pay. You can reasonably conclude that he probably is not going to pay and that you are going to have to persuade him that he should pay.

   Write two letters, using a different appeal in each letter, to convince Mr. Klinker that it is urgent for him to pay the balance of his account. To be effective, each letter must be personalized! Use separate sheets of paper.

FOURTH: THE "YOU MUST PAY" LETTER

The "you must pay" stage is the final stage in the collection series. In this stage, usually one single letter is sent to give the reader a final chance to pay before you take last-resort action, such as turning the account over to an attorney or to a collection agency. Fortunately, most delinquent customers pay or make arrangements to pay before this stage is reached; occasionally, however, some "you must pay" letters have to be written.

Last-resort action for delinquent credit accounts is commonly left to a collection agency. A collection agency uses rigorous collection methods and exchanges information on delinquent customers, which could advertise customers' bad records.

You should attempt to design this final pay-up letter forcefully —with collection talk from beginning to end. Consider the following "you must pay" letter:

Dear Ms. Topper:

   It's in your hands now. Yes, only you can save your credit rating and prevent legal action.

   The last thing I want to do is to put your account in the hands of a collection agency. It isn't a good experience for you or for us, but I'm forced to take this action unless I receive your check for $2,438 by July 10.

   Won't you help us avoid this drastic action by contacting me to discuss what you intend to do. Remember, it's in your hands now.

Sincerely,

This letter is straightforward and forceful and gives the customer one last chance to avoid the unpleasantness and expense of having her account turned over to a collection agency. This writer did not choose to review the transaction as some "you must pay" letters successfully do. Notice that the statement "It's in your hands now" sets the stage for the explanation of what such last-resort action will mean. This letter makes a final pitch for payment and sets the deadline. (The tone is as positive as it can be in such a negative situation—cool and formal, but tactful—and it should produce results.)

WRITING ASSIGNMENT

This is it! This is the last chance for Harold Klinker to avoid the experience of having his account put into the hands of a collection agency. Write an individualized, personal letter giving him his one last chance. Use a separate sheet of paper.

unit 14
WRITING EMPLOYMENT LETTERS

Hazel Rennard wound up the ATAA Seminar with a luncheon meeting at 12:45 p.m. on Friday. Certificates of Completion were issued to each of the participants; and Jackson Morrison, president of the ATAA, gave the closing address. He said: "The ability to express your thoughts clearly and precisely in writing is one of the most sought-after skills in business. I am extremely proud to have been chosen to make the closing talk for a seminar for professional writers. Perhaps you're thinking, what does he mean by *professional* writers? One week in a seminar doesn't make me a pro! But it's true. All of you are professional writers. If your agencies pay you to write letters, memos, and reports, then you're a professional writer."

On her flight back to Chicago, Maria, exhausted after the most rigorous learning experience she had ever had, put on the earphones, pushed her seat back, and closed her eyes. Her mind was a buzz with many new ideas on how to improve communications for World Wide Tours.

On Monday morning, with her bulging attaché case in hand, she went to work an hour early to sort through her many handouts and check her mail before the rest of the staff started trickling in.

Looking through her mail, she found the following interoffice memo:

TO:	**Maria Garcia**	FROM:	**Anne Jacobs**
SUBJECT:	**Junior Correspondent Applications**	DATE:	**February 10, 19—**

Twenty-five applications have come in for the junior correspondent vacancy in your department. The three candidates whose applications are enclosed look good to me, but I'd like you to rank them in the order of the quality of their writing style. Since the candidate selected will be working with you and because you have been trained to be our "resident pro" in letter, memo, and report writing, you can best help me judge the applications.

Let me hear from you today, Maria, as I'll interview the candidates in the order of your recommendations.

Maria chose David A. Van Husen as the first-place winner. Read his letter of application and his résumé, which are shown on pages 148–149 and 154.

How would you react to David's letter? Would you grant him an interview?

David uses one of the most effective approaches to apply for this job. He sends a résumé (a summary of his qualifications) and a letter of application. Of course, the résumé (or data sheet, as it is also called) and the letter are interrelated. This type of application is pleasing and inviting to read. David's letter is of moderate length and makes logical, psychological, and emotional appeals.

Of all the letters that you will have to write, the letter applying for a job will be the most important to you. Your future is at stake. Success or failure here affects your future. Someday, someplace, you will want one job very badly. If the job is worth anything at all, there will be other people applying for it. You will want to impress

5301 Cynthia Lane
Rockford, IL 61109
February 4, 19--

Ms. Anne Jacobs
General Manager
World Wide Tours
7800 Olive Drive
Downers Grove, IL 60515

Dear Ms. Jacobs:

Will you please consider me an applicant for the junior correspondent vacancy in your word processing center that you advertised in the January 27 Evening Star. My enclosed resume, I feel, will support my belief that I am qualified to handle the job.

I will be graduated from East Chicago High School, Chicago, Illinois 60616, on June 16, 19--, and will be ready for employment anytime after that date. While in high school, I maintained a perfect attendance record and a B average. During my senior year, I am participating in our school's Office Education Training Program. Through this special program, I have been able to acquire on-the-job work experience as an assistant sales correspondent for the Vangard Insurance Company, 4500 Michigan Avenue, Chicago, Illinois 60653. Here my duties include taking dictation, transcribing, handling routine correspondence, and managing the appointment book for six sales representatives. In this position, I have discovered an aptitude and liking for writing, and I hope to pursue this aptitude in business.

As you will notice on my resume, I have actively participated in extra-curricular activities. Probably the most challenging activity was our successful attempt to raise $2,000 to carry on our activities in the Future Business Leaders of America club. Club member involvement, teamwork, and responsibility have become more significant to me because of such activities.

Mr. Richard Loo, office manager for Vangard Insurance Company, and the others listed on my resume have given me permission to use their names as references. You may call them or write to them for further information concerning my character and working abilities.

A letter of application helps to match the applicant's qualifications to the employer's needs.

```
        Ms. Anne Jacobs
        February 4, 19--
        Page 2


        Will you please allow me a personal interview?  If you wish, you may call
        me at (312) 555-2805 after 4:30 p.m.

                                      Cordially yours,



                                      David A. Van Husen

        Enclosure
```

the reader. You will want to look your very best. You will want your request to be granted.

This is the real test of your letter-writing abilities. Obviously, you will have to meet all the requirements of the particular job for which you are applying. However, just as important will be your ability to make your letter more impressive than those of the others who are applying. Someone will use your letter and résumé to judge your ability to select the facts, interpret the facts, and set your personality in writing. Your letter and résumé must sell your qualifications for the job.

GETTING THE FACTS FOR YOUR RÉSUMÉ

The first step in attempting to make a job application is to accumulate facts for your résumé. Of course, your résumé should be thorough. Don't overlook anything that is important. Keep in mind that it will be much easier for you to cut down from a large number of facts than it will be for you to add to a skimpy supply. Your résumé should include the five basic categories of information shown on page 150.

Personal
Work experience
Education
Interests, hobbies, and achievements (or Extracurricular)
References

Take a sheet of paper or several 3 by 5 cards and list as much information as you possibly can under each of these five headings. When listing your education and work experience, use reverse chronological order; in other words, list the most recent *first*. When listing other information, place the most significant facts first. This will save you time later when you draft your résumé.

Remember that the résumé is factual and impersonal. As in the sample résumé for David Van Husen, the writer says, "Specialized in business courses," not "*I* specialized in business courses." Incomplete sentences, then, are preferred.

Personal. List your date of birth and your physical condition (height, weight, and general health) in a form such as the following:

PERSONAL

> Date of Birth: May 30, 19—.
> Health: Excellent   Height: 5′6″   Weight: 125

NOTE: You may, if you wish, place this Personal section after your References section.

Work Experience. To have acquired work experience before being graduated from high school is impressive and is worthy of emphasis. Make a survey of your work experience. Are you presently enrolled in a cooperative part-time training program? Do you have experience as a baby-sitter or paper carrier? List each entry, beginning with your most recent position. If you have two or three to list, then omit jobs such as baby-sitter and paper carrier. Be sure to include the title of the job, the name of the employer or company, the address, and the supervisor's name and telephone number.

NOTE: If you have very little or no work experience, you may emphasize your Education and Extracurricular sections by placing both *before* your Experience section.

EXPERIENCE

Accounting clerk. Maryland Natural Gas Company, 2142 Excelsior Boulevard, Rockville, MD 20850. September 19—, to present. Supervisor: Mr. Roy Lind, Telephone: (301) 935-4102.
Clerk. Woolworth's, Knollwood Plaza, Rockville, MD 20850. June 19—, to September 19—. Supervisor: Mrs. Alma Ross, Telephone: (301) 938-3241.

Education. As a high school graduate, it is not necessary for you to list the elementary school or schools that you attended. If you are to be graduated in June of the year you are writing the letter, you should say "Will be graduated from East Chicago High School, Chicago, Illinois 60616, on June 4, 19—." If you have already been graduated, you can say "Was graduated from. . . ." (Do not say "Will graduate" or "Graduated from," because only an institution has the power to graduate. Say "Will *be* graduated from" or "*Was* graduated from.") You should also indicate the performance level you attained in courses that directly relate to the job. See the examples in the Education section shown below.

EDUCATION

Will be graduated from East Chicago High School, Chicago, Illinois 60616, on June 4, 19—.
Attained an A− average in business classes.
Specialized in business subjects and attained:

1. **Typewriting speed of 70 + words per minute.**
2. **Shorthand speed of 140 words per minute.**
3. **Ability to operate the following business machines: Dictaphone, Selectric typewriter, IBM Memory, and the IBM System 6.**

Have been accepted by Chicago Community College, Chicago, Illinois 60605.

Also, in the Education section be sure to list any special honors, awards, or achievements, such as the honor roll or the National Honor Society.

If you are listing more than one school which you have attended (not counting elementary schools), place them in reverse chronological order with the most recent school listed first.

_____ **Interests, Hobbies, and Achievements.** Most employers look for well-rounded individuals, applicants who are compatible with others and who have good leadership ability. Include in your résumé any activities that will show a prospective employer that you are well rounded and that you will get along well with others.

Actually there are two types of student activities that you may list: (1) Co-curricular—those that are related directly to classroom instruction, like the vocational youth organizations (Office Education Association, Distributive Education Clubs of America, Future Business Leaders of America, Vocational Industrial Clubs of America, Future Farmers of America, and Future Homemakers of America); and (2) Extracurricular—those not directly related to classroom instruction (sports, chorus, debate, and so on). See the following example:

INTERESTS, HOBBIES, AND ACHIEVEMENTS

Vice president of the East Chicago Chapter of Illinois Office Education Association.
Student secretary for Office Coordinator.
Member of Donaldson's Teen Board.
Junior volunteer at Fairview Hospital.
Member of 19— School Yearbook staff.
Hobbies of skiing and reading.

_____ **References.** Consider three or four references _other than relatives_ who can speak well of you. Get permission from them to use their names as references _before_ listing them. If the person you ask is quick to accept, you can usually assume that you've got a good reference.

Employers usually place great importance on the recommendations made by people who have seen your job performance, so if possible, be sure to list the name of someone for whom you have worked. It is also wise to list at least one member of your school staff, as employers invariably check with your school about your high school record. Include no more than one personal or character reference. When listing your references, be sure to include their complete names, describe their positions, give their business addresses, and give their telephone numbers. Make it as easy as possible for the person reading your qualifications to contact your references. Those writers who say "references provided upon request" are merely delaying their getting the job. Most employers prefer having this information on the résumé.

REFERENCES

Mrs. Edna Lansing, Engineering Manager, Midwest Construction Company, 4820 West Pierson Road, Flint, MI 48504, (313) 927-9981.

Mr. Allen Yoder, Manager, Barstow Industries, 8402 Jackson Court, Jackson, MI 49201, (517) 938-1170.

Once you have compiled a listing of all your qualifications and have double-checked to see that you have included all the facts and all the pertinent information, you are ready to summarize these qualifications for your résumé.

WRITING ASSIGNMENT

Using 3 by 5 cards, list all the facts you can about yourself. As suggested previously in the chapter, use one or more cards for each of the five main headings.

USING THE FACTS TO WRITE THE RÉSUMÉ	To be effective, the résumé must be visually attractive. It should be well organized and show an orderly presentation if it is to command the reader's attention.

Individually type each résumé on 8½-by 11-inch, 20-pound, white bond paper. Never use a carbon copy! If you need more than a few copies, ask a small-job printer how much it would cost to print 50 or 100 copies.

Begin your résumé with a well-displayed heading containing your name, address, and telephone number. Then you must decide upon the overall sequence of the topics. As already stated, the order should be from the most important to the least important.

Really try to limit yourself to one page! Since a résumé is a summary, it should be short; so reevaluate your facts and delete irrelevant material. Just as lengthy letters are burdensome, so are lengthy résumés. Use a two-page résumé only if you feel you *must* to include all your qualifications.

David A. Van Husen
5301 Cynthia Lane
Rockford, IL 61109
(312) 555-2805

PERSONAL

Date of Birth: August 8, 19--
Health: Excellent   Height: 5'11"   Weight: 149

EXPERIENCE

Assistant sales correspondent. Vangard Insurance Company, 4500 Michigan Avenue, Chicago, Illinois 60653. September 19-- to present. Supervisor: Ms. Anna Robinson. Telephone: (312) 427-9530, Extension 419.

Kitchen aid. McCarthy's Catering, 93 West Mill Road, Rockford, Illinois 61104. September 19-- to June 19--. Supervisor: Mr. Maurice Doher. Telephone: (312) 210-4987, Extension 2167.

EDUCATION

Will be graduated from East Chicago High School, Chicago, IL 60616, in June 19--.

Participated in the Office Education Training Program in senior year. Specialized in business courses and attained:

1. Typewriting speed, 60 wpm; shorthand speed, 120 wpm.
2. An understanding and operating knowledge of transcribing machines, IBM Magnetic Tape Selectric, and IBM System 6.
3. A working knowledge of electronic calculators; ten-key adding machines; and fluid, mimeograph, and offset duplicators.
4. An understanding of human relations with co-workers and with superiors and subordinates.

Maintained a B average at East Chicago High School.

EXTRACURRICULAR

Member of Chicago Chapter of Illinois Office Education Association.
Member of Illinois Chapter of Future Business Leaders of America.
Chairperson of Future Business Leaders of America Fund Raising Drive to raise $2,000 for club activities.
Member of Y-Teen at East Chicago High School for last two years.

REFERENCES

Mrs. Vi Gislason, Office Education Coordinator, East Chicago High School, 4398 West 22 Street, Chicago, IL 60616, (312) 431-9208.

Mr. Richard Loo, Office Manager, Vangard Insurance Company, 4500 Michigan Avenue, Chicago, IL 60653, (312) 427-9530.

Mrs. Martha Ellsworth, homemaker, 4120 Butterworth Heights, Elgin, IL 60120, (312) 245-9835.

Ms. Jennifer Best, Principal, East Chicago High School, 4398 West 22 Street, Chicago, IL 60616, (312) 431-9208.

A résumé is a summary of an applicant's qualifications for employment.

For good eye appeal, allow ample space and use clear headings and subheadings for groups and subgroups of data. Express parallel items in a parallel manner; for example:

Member of Missouri Chapter of Distributive Education Clubs of America.
Student secretary for Office Coordinator.
Editor of 19— School Yearbook.

You would not say in the last entry "*Was* editor of . . ." because "*Was* editor" is not parallel to "Member" and to "Student secretary." And remember to use phrases rather than sentences.

WRITING ASSIGNMENT

Recheck your 3 by 5 cards to make sure you haven't forgotten any pertinent information. Then use these cards to draft a complete, orderly, attractive résumé. (Use the illustration on page 156 as your guide.) Check your draft for any final corrections; then type the résumé neatly on good-quality, 8½-by 11-inch paper. Limit it to one page, but make it interesting.

USING THE RÉSUMÉ EFFECTIVELY

If your final résumé is well prepared and complete, it will serve several purposes. First, your résumé will be very helpful during an interview. Even if you have sent the interviewer your résumé, bring another copy with you to the interview. When you introduce yourself to the interviewer, you could say: "Hello, Mr. Struthers. I'm Pat Smith. I'm applying for the secretarial vacancy in the research lab. I've compiled this résumé. Maybe it can be of some help to you in our interview." And be sure to bring a copy for yourself! Second, your résumé will serve as a fact sheet that you can use to fill out the company's application form. All the dates, names, and addresses that you will need are listed in your résumé. Third, this résumé will serve as the basis for your future résumés.

WRITING THE LETTER OF APPLICATION

After you have decided on the job you would like to apply for, you should learn as much as you can about the job and the *firm*. (Can you imagine anyone applying for a job and not knowing such general facts as the location of the firm, job requirements, salary range, opportunity for advancement, and so on?) To make a preliminary investigation, call the company's personnel office (if practical in terms of distance), arrange a conversation with an employee of the firm, or read the job advertisement very carefully (some of these ads thoroughly describe the job opening). Many companies have brochures that will be helpful to you.

The more preliminary investigating you do, the more effective your letter will be and the better you will be able to sell your product—you. A blind approach to a job application can be as unsuccessful as attempting to sell a product to a public about which you know nothing. How can you write persuasively and make logical, psychological, and emotional appeals unless you know your market—the prospective employer? Your attempt to learn something about the prospective employer will show that you have initiative —a desirable characteristic for any prospective employee.

With this information and your résumé, you are ready to write a good sales letter—your letter of application. Here comes the real test of your letter-writing abilities: a descriptive, explanatory, and highly persuasive letter.

Listing the facts for your résumé forced you to accumulate much information about yourself. Getting the preliminary facts about the job and your prospective employer has provided you with information concerning the requirements of the position that you are seeking. All this vital information will help you to *match* these job requirements to the qualifications you possess.

If the letter makes such a match obvious to your reader, you will be enthusiastically considered for an interview. After all, you are in demand. The employer needs you if you can do the job. Your résumé can serve as the job-qualification fact sheet; however, it should be your *letter* that will sell your prospective employer on the fact that you have the qualifications necessary to fill the job. The match must be obvious; it cannot be left to chance. Your letter must tell exactly how your qualifications actually meet the job requirements.

You must sell your reader on your product—you. In the letter of application, match your qualifications to the employer's needs. With this approach, you are bound to land the job!

The Format of the Letter. Will you succeed in convincing your prospective employer that you are the best person for the job? To be sure you do succeed, follow these suggestions in writing your letter:

1. Attract favorable attention by:
   a. Taking pains with the physical appearance and arrangement of the letter (stationery, typing, paragraphing, grammar, punctuation, spelling, and so on).
   b. Explaining how you learned of the vacancy, if possible.
   c. Indicating the exact purpose of the letter.

> **Mrs. Janice Sullivan, my office coordinator, has informed me of a secretarial vacancy in your firm. Will you please consider me an enthusiastic applicant?**

2. Create desire or interest by:
   a. Stating and then analyzing the major requirements of the position you have in mind.
   b. Showing conclusively that your education, training, and experience specifically meet these requirements. Remember that your résumé is attached to the letter and should be referred to throughout the letter. It isn't necessary, however, for you to repeat in your letter all the facts that are on your résumé. Consistently *lead* the reader into the résumé for actual facts.

> **As you will see on my enclosed résumé, since last year I have been working part-time as a clerk-typist for Data Tronics, Inc.**

3. Convince the employer that you are the person for the job by:
   a. Supplementing the statement already made with a presentation of those personal qualifications or characteristics that seem most desirable.

> **During my senior year, I was elected vice president of the Miami Chapter of the Future Business Leaders of America. By working to gain the support and team effort of my peers, I have become conscious of the importance of good human relations. This awareness should make me a more qualified and perceptive secretary.**

   b. Showing genuine interest in the business and expressing confidence in your ability to adapt your particular training to meet the employer's requirements.
   c. Suggesting, if it seems appropriate, your ultimate career goal, as well as your immediate objective.

    d. Reassuring the employer that you don't want just work, but rather the chance to tackle a given problem and solve it.

4. Stimulate action by:
    a. Offering references that will vouch for your experience, education, and character.
    b. Requesting an interview.
    c. Supplying the employer with the information necessary to arrange the interview.

> **To arrange an interview at your convenience, please call me at Data Tronics from 3 p.m. to 6 p.m. any day from Monday through Friday.**

The Beginning of the Letter. The first paragraph of the letter of application should immediately arouse the reader's attention. If the letter fails here, it usually fails in its ultimate purpose—to get you an interview. Most employers judge the ability of an applicant by the degree of excellence of this letter.

    Your first paragraph should suggest your individuality. Avoid trite, hackneyed beginnings, and do not be too radical, eccentric, or artificial. The beginning should reveal the purpose of your letter and indicate how you learned about the position. Do not be vague. Do not leave it to the reader to guess the purpose of your letter.

WRITING ASSIGNMENT

Write the first paragraph of a letter of application for each of the following situations. In each case, fill in the specific details required.

1. Assume that a friend—not known to the reader—told you about a job opening in a company for which you would like to work.

_____

_____

_____

_____

_____

_____

_____

2. Assume that a friend of yours—an expert who is well known in your field and is highly respected by the reader—told you about the job.

_____

_____

_____

_____

_____

_____

_____

The Middle of the Letter. In the middle section of your letter, develop the relation of your education and experience (if you have any) to the requirements of the position. To stress your best selling points, place them in the most prominent position.

In the middle section, be sure to include:

1. A presentation of the particular requirements of the position.
2. A detailed account of your education and your practical work experience.
3. A convincing statement _matching_ your particular qualifications to the specific requirements of the position. (This is the _match_ we discussed, and it is probably the most important part of your letter. It shows why you have an interest in the position.)

Your letter must reveal your ambition, your determination, and your abilities. Your positive traits and skills are what the employer is looking for. If your interests and hobbies describe you better than anything else, then use them to describe yourself. But do not make the body of the letter too long or involved. Each paragraph should emphasize a particular selling point. Sentences should be clear and to the point. Avoid all irrelevant material.

The End of the Letter. The end or conclusion of your letter of application has a twofold purpose—to request an interview and to make it easy for the reader to grant that interview. Leave no doubt in the reader's mind of your desire for an interview. State definitely and completely how and when you may be reached. Give as much attention to the individuality and the force of your ending as you do to the beginning of your letter.

WRITING ASSIGNMENT

From the want ads in your local newspaper, choose a job for which you would like to apply and for which you are qualified. If you prefer, you may choose as your potential job an opening described to you by a friend. In either case, get as many facts as possible about the potential job and the employer. Then, using the résumé you prepared, write a persuasive letter of application. Type your letter of application on plain bond paper, 8½ by 11 inches. Do not use printed letterhead for letters of application.

WRITING A FOLLOW-UP LETTER

After an interview, some applicants write a letter to thank the interviewer. People who conduct interviews admit frankly that they are impressed when they receive such letters and that they don't receive enough of them. Obviously, you probably won't be considered for the job just because you wrote it, but your follow-up letter could have some bearing in a very close contest between you and another applicant.

This letter must be prompt and sincere. It should be written on the same day as the interview or no later than the day following the interview. It should reach the reader before he or she has made a decision.

Here is an example of a follow-up letter:

Thank you for giving me a chance to talk to you in person about my qualifications for the junior correspondent vacancy in your word processing unit. Also, I certainly appreciated meeting your general manager, Ms. Ann Jacobs. Now I know why World Wide Tours is Number 1 in the nation in wholesale travel sales.

This experience made me even more eager to work with all of you. I look forward to hearing from you about the job.

This letter is not gushy. Appropriately, it shows appreciation for having been granted an interview (not for the time spent in the interview) and for having been introduced to the general manager.

WRITING ASSIGNMENT

Yesterday you had an interview with Mrs. Agatha Cushing, personnel manager for Cardinal Industries. She told you that although no jobs were now available, she would be glad to have you call again in two or three months. As you left her office, Mrs. Cushing gave you a booklet describing the company and its products. Write a letter thanking her for the interview in a way that will make her think favorably of you and will remind her of you when a person with your qualifications is needed. Such letters are interpreted as evidence of good manners.

_____

_____

_____

_____

_____

_____

_____

_____

_____

WRITING A LETTER OF RESIGNATION

Another employment letter that you may have to write is a resignation letter. As a business worker you must give your employer formal notice that you plan to leave the company, and you should give this notice at least two weeks before you will leave. Look at the illustration below.

Dear Mr. Brooks:

Please accept my resignation as executive secretary for the Research Department effective June 10, 19—.

Since I plan to move to Denver, Colorado, on July 1, I will need a few weeks to get things ready and packed. If you wish, I will be happy to train my replacement.

Thank you for the opportunity to work with your Research Department. This job allowed me to expand my experience and thus become a more perceptive secretary. My replacement has much to look forward to!

Respectfully yours,

This letter of resignation:

1. Is brief and to the point.
2. States the specific date of termination.
3. States the reasons for terminating employment. (You should use tact in stating reasons. For instance, you should not say, "I am taking a position with the Spoon River Company because it pays more money." "Personal advancement" is one acceptable reason that is noncommittal.)
4. Mentions that working with the company has been enjoyable.
5. Uses an appropriate complimentary close, "Respectfully yours."

unit 15
PREPARING FORMAL AND INFORMAL REPORTS

Late one Friday afternoon, Anne dropped into Maria's office and said: "Maria, I need your help. I have just read Jennie Lewiston's sales report, and it is deplorable. The content is not that bad, but it is so poorly organized and loosely written that I almost lost the message. Do you think that you can make a study of the problem and recommend a plan of action for us to improve reports in our agency?"

Somewhat shocked and yet slightly honored, Maria said: "I can try, Anne. Hazel gave us plenty of material on report writing, and her three-hour session was one of the best of the whole seminar. How about if I get something together and put it in writing for you?"

A smile covered Anne's face as she said: "Great! I knew I could count on you. I guess the thing I appreciate most about you, Maria, is your genuine enthusiasm for new responsibility."

That afternoon Maria pulled out her seminar file and took out all the report writing materials. She knew what she would be doing this weekend.

The first thing Maria did was read through the background material. Let's read along with her.

THE NEED FOR REPORTS

Every organization, profit-making and non-profit-making, sets goals that it must reach each year. A manufacturing company or a retail store chain, for example, will try to increase its business each year by selling more products more profitably. A non-profit-making organization such as Community Fund or the United Way will try to raise more money every year and to use that money more productively to improve and expand the services it offers to communities. Whether the organization is profit-making or not, its management must make key decisions that will determine how well the organization reaches its goals. These decisions will concern costs and expenses, advertising and marketing strategies, personnel policies, and so on.

To make wise decisions, management must rely on the useful information it receives from its employees, and one of the most useful sources of information is the business report.

A written report is a common, yet a most important, means of communicating valuable information to other members of the organization. The report may be short or it may be long. It may be written on a periodic basis (once a week, once a month, once a year), or it may be a special report written for a specific purpose. It may simply require the writer to compile and organize some dates, prices, or other statistics that are readily available, or it may require a year-long research and a detailed analysis and interpretation of statistics, perhaps offering suggestions and recommendations of monumental importance. However one report may differ from another, all reports share this common goal: to communicate reliable, useful information to other members of the organization.

Note the key word *useful*. In business we judge reports by their usefulness. The more useful the information, the better the report.

To simplify our discussion of reports, let's separate them into two categories: formal (or analytical) reports and informal reports.

WRITING FORMAL REPORTS	Sometimes "putting things in writing" calls for more than short memorandum reports. Such reports as progress reports, performance analysis reports, market reports, periodic reports, and stockholders' reports deserve careful investigation in order to present and analyze important data and to develop a plan of action. Analytical reports like these are formal in organization and in content. When you prepare such formal reports, you will need to (1) state the purpose of your report, (2) get the facts for your report, and (3) make an outline for your report.

State the purpose of your report. The purpose of the use of your report must be clear to you before you gather your data. Your purpose should state why the report is written and who asked for it. For example, the purpose of Maria's report said:

This report, prepared for all department heads at the request of Anne Jacobs, assesses the report writing training needs at World Wide Tours, presents possible training recommendations, and suggests courses of action for department heads to follow in order to improve the reports prepared in their departments.

Get the facts for your report. Once Maria clearly stated the purpose of her report, she confirmed it with Anne. They both agreed that it was on target. Having agreed upon the purpose, Maria proceeded to gather the facts. She decided to gather information from the following sources: (1) Anne Jacobs (the person at World Wide to whom most of the reports are submitted), (2) the heads of the sales and promotion, accounting, credit, and personnel departments, (3) persons within the organization who have written good reports, (4) her file from the ATAA Seminar, and (5) communication teachers.

To get the facts for her report, Maria read and read and read. Using the brief questionnaire she developed, she interviewed each of her sources and took many notes on their responses.

—————————— **Make an outline for your report.** A formal report outline should include (1) the purpose of the report, (2) the need for the report, (3) the introduction and findings of the report, and (4) the conclusions and recommendations of the report.

Once the purpose of the report has been agreed upon, the report writer needs to describe the circumstances that have brought about the request for it. Maria's need statement could begin as follows:

NEED: **Employees of World Wide Tours write about 15 formal reports each month. The information provided in these reports is used as the basis for key management decisions.**

If World Wide Tours is to continue to grow, better and better reports will need to be generated so that better expansion decisions can be made.

Presently, World Wide Tours reports are written and organized inconsistently, and . . . .

Once the need is stated, the report writing is ready to provide a description of how the facts were gathered. Maria's introduction could begin as follows:

INTRODUCTION: **The information gathered for this report was compiled by reviewing readings and by interviewing the following: . . .**

The findings of the report will be written from the notes that were taken when gathering the facts. (As in theme writing, 3 by 5 cards may be used to take notes, with one card for each fact.) The findings, of course, will have a great bearing on the conclusions and recommendations. In Maria's conclusions she wrote:

1. **The findings suggest that there is a definite need for report writing training.**

2. **The above findings suggest the following options for training World Wide Tours personnel: . . .**

Then she listed her recommendations.

It is recommended that:

1. **A detailed in-service training program in report writing be given to all department heads.**

2. **Short training sessions be provided for other employees involved in report writing.**

3. **A report writing manual for agency employees be developed.**

4. **All first-draft reports be reviewed for format with the senior correspondent of the Word Processing Center before the final version is prepared.**

Because of the complexity and the length of most formal reports, they are generally divided into the following parts:

Title Page. This is the first page of the formal report and usually includes four things: the title, the name of the person receiving the report, the author, and the date the report is submitted. Of course, all these things should be arranged attractively. Never type a page number on a title page. The title is usually centered in capital letters and should be as concise as possible.

Preface. The preface is an introductory discussion. In it, the author may give background material, reasons for undertaking the project, the method of conducting research, and so on. A roman numeral is used to number the preface page.

Table of Contents. This is a list of what will follow in the text of the report. The contents includes the titles of the sections of the report and of the major headings within each section. Each section and heading title is typed on a separate line. As in the table of contents of a printed book, a corresponding page number is typed next to each line to show where the section begins. A roman numeral is also used on each page of the table of contents.

List of Illustrations. The list of illustrations helps the reader locate visual and graphic aids by listing the page numbers on which they appear. Again, a roman numeral is used to number this page.

Synopsis (or Abstract). The synopsis is a summary of the text. Its length may vary, but it should include a statement of the problem, your findings, and your conclusions or recommendations. The purpose of placing the summary before the actual text is to rapidly relay the message of the report to your reader. This section, too, is paginated in roman numerals.

Body or Text. This is the main section of the formal report. Here the subject is explained and analyzed. An introduction, including a statement of the purpose of the report and perhaps the methods used in gathering facts, opens the body of the report. This is followed by a discussion, an analysis, and a presentation of the facts. A conclusion or summary ends this part of the report.

Beginning with the body or text, arabic numbers will be used throughout the rest of the report. Since the rules of typing reports state that no number is typed on the first page, start with arabic numeral 2 on the second page of the report.

Appendix. This supplementary section contains graphic aids that would be too cumbersome if inserted in the body of the report. (For example, Maria's questionnaire could be included here so that the interested reader could see how the writer gathered her information.) Material that is less than one-half of a page should be included in the text rather than in the appendix. The reader should not be asked to flip to the appendix for constant reference.

Bibliography. The bibliography is a list of the books and periodicals used as sources of information in writing the report. (For example, Maria's seminar materials would be mentioned in her bibliography, as well as any reference manuals that report writers might find helpful.) For each entry, include the author's name, the title of the article, the name of the book or periodical, the volume and issue number, the name of the publisher, the place of publication, and the date of publication. This listing should be in alphabetical order by authors' surnames.

Index. The index, the final supplementary section, is an alphabetical listing of the significant names, topics, and subtopics contained in the report, together with a notation of the pages on which each appears throughout the report.

Formal reports are usually bound. Depending upon the importance of the report, it can be bound in beautiful covers with spiral binding or three-hole-punched and placed in a folder-type report binding or in a loose-leaf book. For a guide to typing your report, see *The Gregg Reference Manual, Fifth Edition,* by William A. Sabin, McGraw-Hill, New York, 1977.

Letter of Transmittal. Bound formal reports require a letter of transmittal, which is a covering letter or a memo that accompanies each copy of the report. Maria's letter of transmittal read as follows:

TO:	Anne Jacobs	FROM:	Maria Garcia
SUBJECT:	Report on "Report Writing"	DATE:	March 21, 19—

As promised, I am attaching a copy of my report, "Improving Report Writing Practices at World Wide Travel," prepared for you at your request. I certainly hope that the report is useful to you in making your decision regarding the course of action that should be taken to improve the quality of reports submitted by our department heads.

May I meet with you at your convenience to discuss the report? I will be happy to answer any questions you may have regarding its contents.

cc Allison Williams, Sales and Promotion
　Bill Jo Zimmerman, Accounting
　Shirley Shannon, Personnel
　Joe Rocco, Credit

WRITING ASSIGNMENT

You work in the Purchasing Department for a large manufacturing firm in your area. For years, your firm has bought cars for its 100 sales representatives throughout the country. Now the director of purchasing, Mr. Jonathon Majors, wants to investigate the feasibility of leasing cars from a dealer, and he asks you to study the possibility, gather the relevant information, and make recommendations based on your findings. On a separate sheet of paper, write the report, as well as a covering letter, for Mr. Majors.

In your report, be sure to provide the comparisons between present costs of buying cars and estimated costs of leasing cars. Make up all cost figures, assuming that you have several years worth of data on file for buying cars. Use a newspaper to find realistic costs of leasing cars, or call a local dealer (use your telephone directory to find the names of car-leasing agencies in your area).

WRITING INFORMAL REPORTS	Most of the reports that you will write will simply provide factual information about a subject. These informal reports are most common when research is light and where content is brief. The two formats for informal reports are the *memorandum* (used for communications within the company) and the *letter* (used for communications to other companies). A sample memorandum report appears on page 172. The letter report contains all the elements of a regular business letter—heading, inside address, salutation, body, closing, and signature.

When you prepare an informal report, using either the memorandum or the letter format, you may wish to make a continuous flow of the content of the text; or if it is too lengthy or cumbersome, you may wish to attach separate sheets to the report in the form of enclosures. This will depend on the length and the nature of your information. You will also have to choose either a personal tone (*I, you*) or an impersonal tone (*the writer* and *the reader* instead of *I* and *you*), depending on your reader. The personal tone is usually preferred.

Whether your report is a letter or a memorandum, you will have to decide how you are going to present your information. You may wish to present your data in alphabetical order, order of importance, chronological order—whichever serves your purpose best.

_____ **Alphabetic order.** If you were asked, for example, to prepare an up-to-date list of the service centers that your company operates throughout the country, you might arrange your information as follows:

> **Abilene, Texas 79603**
> **Abilene Appliance Center, 112 Main Street**
> **Albany, New York 12210**
> **Capitol Service, 8 Utica Avenue**
> **Albuquerque, New Mexico 87111**
> **Southwest Appliance Service, 1162 Sunset Highway**
> **Baltimore, Maryland 21215**
> **Authorized Service Center, 432 Route 79**
> **Better Service Center, 80 Avenue T**
> **Canton, Ohio 44702**
> **Professional Appliance Services, 57 Lowell Boulevard**

_____ **Order of importance.** If, for example, you were asked to compare the sales of various products for one full year, you might arrange your data according to their importance—that is, according to their dollar sales.

PRODUCT	UNIT SALES	DOLLAR SALES
UltraJoy Liquid Cleaner (quart), $1.98	**96,241**	**$190,557**
Brite Shine Polish, $1.69	**82,431**	**138,308**
UltraJoy Liquid Cleaner (gallon), $4.98	**26,642**	**132,677**
Silver-Glo Spray, $2.29	**51,439**	**117,795**

_____ **Chronological order.** Say, for example, that your company advertises in several monthly magazines. The advertising manager wants to know exactly how many of the coupon order forms that accompany these ads have been received for each magazine ad since the beginning of this year. You decide to present the information in chronological order.

MONTH	FUN MAGAZINE	RSVP MAGAZINE	REALITIES MAGAZINE	MONTHLY TOTAL
January	65	78	94	237
February	56	83	106	245
March	89	57	86	232
April	98	87	94	279
TOTAL	308	305	380	993

Notice the following example of a routine information report. This particular report lists the information in chronological order.

TO: **Daniel Evans**   FROM: **Pat Kramer**
SUBJECT: **Estimated Sales Compared**   DATE: **June 12, 19—**
With Actual Sales for The
Art of Writing Effective
Letters, Second Edition

In answer to your June 9 request, I have compared the estimated sales figures with the actual sales figures for The Art of Writing Effective Letters, by Stein and Robinson, since its publication.

SALES	19—	19—	19—	19—	TOTAL
Number of copies					
Estimated	10,000	11,000	10,500	10,000	41,500
Actual	7,800	14,000	13,800	15,000	50,600
Dollar revenue					
Estimated	$60,000	$66,000	$63,000	$60,000	$249,000
Actual	$46,800	$84,000	$82,800	$90,000	$303,600

Although actual sales fell below estimated sales for the first year, actual sales were greater than estimated sales for each succeeding year. Thus the total actual sales to date exceeds estimated sales by 9,100 copies, or $54,600.

Please let me know if you would like to see a complete profit study for this edition or a comparison of sales with the previous edition.

This is an effective informal report because:

1. The subject is clearly stated in the first paragraph.
2. It gives the reader the information requested. It contains no irrelevant information and offers to provide more information if the reader wishes it.
3. It presents the information in an easy-to-understand manner. The tabular display makes it easy for the reader to compare estimated sales with actual sales for each year. Presenting the information in sentence form would have made it more difficult to compare these figures.
4. The use of the pronouns *I, you,* and *me* gives it a direct but personal flavor.

WRITING ASSIGNMENT

Your employer, Miss Libby Frank (whom you call by her first name), asks you to prepare a report of the employment anniversary dates of those employees of the Accounting Department whose employment anniversaries fall during the second half of the year. To get this information you search the personnel files and secure the following information.

Roosevelt Brown, a payroll clerk, was hired 4 years ago on August 23; Janis Johnson, a billing clerk, has been with the company for 18 years and was hired on November 19; Myron Shapiro, an accounts receivable clerk, started with the company 7 years ago on October 6; Lawrence Laguri, an accounts payable clerk, will celebrate his 10th anniversary with the company on December 29.

On a separate sheet of paper, write an informal memorandum report to Miss Frank, presenting this information in a clear, easy-to-understand manner. Be sure to include the headings *To, From, Subject,* and *Date,* as in the memorandum on page 172.

REFERENCE SECTION

Your written messages must meet the standards of modern business correspondence. Whenever you are uncertain whether your punctuation, number, abbreviation, or capitalization style is correct, find the right answer in an authoritative source. The short time that it will take you to do so will be well worth the effort!

This Reference Section includes a summary of the most commonly used principles of punctuation, number, abbreviation, and capitalization styles for business writing. Read this section to become acquainted with these principles, and refer to it whenever you must. For a complete manual on grammar, usage, and style, see *The Gregg Reference Manual, Fifth Edition, by William A. Sabin.** The material in this Reference Section has been condensed from that book.

PUNCTUATION

The Period

1. Use a period to mark the end of a sentence that makes a statement or expresses a command.

> **Margaret Jackson has been promoted to vice president of marketing. (Statement.)**
>
> **Be sure to return the contract promptly. (Command.)**

2. Use a period to mark the end of an indirect question.

> **Mr. Hernandez asked me if the report would be ready on time.**

* William A. Sabin, *The Gregg Reference Manual,* 5th ed., Gregg Division, McGraw-Hill Book Company, New York, 1977.

> **Who the new director will be has not yet been announced.**

The Question Mark

1. Use a question mark at the end of a direct question.

> **Where are the notes from yesterday's conference?**
>
> **Why not make an appointment today?**

2. Use a question mark at the end of a sentence that is phrased like a statement but spoken with the rising intonation of a question.

> **They still doubt our figures?**
>
> **The report is not ready yet?**

3. A series of brief questions at the end of a sentence may be separated by commas or (for emphasis) by question marks. Do not capitalize the individual questions.

> **Can you estimate the cost of the roofing, the tile work, and the painting?**
>
> **OR: Can you estimate the cost of the roofing? the tile work? the painting?**

The Exclamation Point

1. Use an exclamation point at the end of a sentence (or an expression that stands for a sentence) to indicate enthusiasm, surprise, incredulity, urgency, or strong feeling.

> **The new advertising art is beautiful!**

2. A single word may be followed by an exclamation point to express intense feeling. The sentence that follows it is punctuated as usual.

Wait! I forgot to put a stamp on the letter.

3. When such words are repeated for emphasis, an exclamation point follows each repetition.

Hush! Hush! Don't let this secret out.

The Comma

The comma has two primary functions: it *separates* elements within a sentence to clarify their relationship to one another, and it *sets off* nonessential elements that interrupt the flow of thought. It takes only a single comma to "separate," but it typically requires two commas to "set off."

1. *In Compound Sentences.* When a compound sentence consists of two independent clauses joined by *and, but, or,* or *nor,* a "separating" comma should precede the conjunction.

Mr. Elliot waited for two hours, *and* **then he announced his decision.**

The material in this coat is not the right color, *nor* **is it the quality ordered.**

2. If the two clauses of a compound sentence are short, the comma may be omitted before the conjunction.

Cathy Harf was correct and her staff knew it.

Please sign these forms and return them by tomorrow.

3. *In Complex Sentences.* A complex sentence contains one independent clause and one or more dependent clauses. *After, although, as, because, before, if, since, unless, when,* and *while* are among the words most frequently used to introduce dependent clauses.

4. When a dependent clause *precedes* a main clause, separate the two clauses with a comma.

Before you decide, **please read this.**

5. When a dependent clause *follows* the main clause or *falls within* the main clause, commas are used or omitted depending on whether the dependent clause is essential (restrictive) or nonessential (nonrestrictive).

a. An *essential* clause is necessary to the meaning of the sentence. Because it *cannot be omitted*, it should not be set off by commas.

This schedule is for everyone *who works in the plant.* **(Tells which persons.)**

Ben said *that the settlement would be hard to reach.* **(Tells what he said.)**

b. A *nonessential* clause provides additional descriptive or explanatory detail. Because it *can be omitted* without changing the meaning of the sentence, it should be set off by commas.

We stopped off in Denver to see our partner, *who is an eminent author.* **(Simply adds information about the partner.)**

c. A dependent clause occurring within a sentence must always be set off by commas when it interrupts the flow of the sentence.

I will send a check for the order, *if that is all right with you,* **on the first of the month.**

6. *With Participial, Infinitive, and Prepositional Phrases.* Use a comma after an *introductory participial phrase.*

Speaking in a loud voice, **Mrs. Earnest called the meeting to order.**

7. Use a comma after an *introductory infinitive phrase* unless the phrase is the subject of the sentence. (Infinitive phrases are introduced by the word *to.*)

To get ahead in this corporation, **you must work hard.**

8. Use a comma after an *introductory prepositional phrase* unless the phrase is short and no misunderstanding is likely to result from the omission of the comma.

In response to the the many requests of our customers, **we are opening a suburban branch. (Comma required after a long phrase.)**

9. *With Introductory, Parenthetical, or Transitional Expressions.* Use commas to set off parenthetical elements—that is, words, phrases, or clauses that are not necessary to the completeness of the structure or the meaning of the sentence. Such expressions either provide a transition from one thought to the next or reflect the writer's attitude toward the meaning of the sentence.

After all, **we have revised these estimates twice.**

The stockholders, *I am sure,* **will be happy with this year's profits.**

10. *In a Series.* When the last member of a series of three or more items is preceded by *and, or,* or *nor,* place a comma before the conjunction as well as between the other items.

Study the rules for the use of the comma, the semicolon, *and* **the colon.**

11. *With Adjectives.* When two or more consecutive adjectives modify the same noun, separate the adjectives by commas.

The agency described her as a *quiet, efficient* **worker. (A worker who is quiet and efficient.)**

12. *With Identifying, Appositive, or Explanatory Expressions.* Words, phrases, and clauses that identify or explain other terms should be set off by commas.

Richard Donahue, *the new financial analyst,* **is revising these procedures.**

13. *With Interruptions of Thought and Afterthoughts.* Use commas to set off words, phrases, or clauses that interrupt the flow of a sentence or that are loosely added at the end as an afterthought.

She has approved, *so I was told,* **the site for our convention.**

14. *To Indicate Omitted Words.* Use a comma to indicate the omission of a word or words that are clearly understood from the context. (The omitted words are usually verbs.)

Sandra Lopes manages our California office; Sal Margot, our Florida office.

15. *In Direct Address.* Names and titles used in direct address must be set off by commas.

Ms. Podolsky, **could you please reschedule the meeting for next Thursday?**

16. *In Dates.* Use two commas to set off the year in month-day-year dates. When only the month and year are given, the growing trend is to omit the commas.

We introduced the product to potential investors on *January 2, 1981,* **as we were scheduled to.**

Mr. Cutler joined our firm in *April 1980.*

17. *With States and Countries.* Use two commas to set off the name of a state, a country, a county, etc., that directly follows a city name.

Karen Robinson's trip took her to St. Louis, *Missouri,* **and then to Tokyo,** *Japan.*

18. *With* Jr. *and* Sr. Use commas to set off *Jr.* and *Sr.* if you know that this is the person's preference. However, the growing trend is to omit the commas.

Mr. L. B. Kelly, *Jr.,* **is our district manager in this area.**

19. *With* Esq., *Academic Degrees, Religious Orders.* Abbreviations like *Esq.* and those that stand for academic degrees or religious orders are set off by two commas.

Janet Lee, *Ph.D.*, will address the Conservation Club on Thursday, January 4.

20. *With* Inc. *and* Ltd. The growing trend is to omit the commas with *Inc., Ltd.,* and similar expressions in company names. However, always follow a company's preference when you know what it is.

Scarpa Shoes, Ltd. (company's preference) BUT: Time Inc.

21. *In Figures.* When numbers run to four or more figures, use commas to separate thousands, hundreds of thousands, millions, etc.

$2,375.88   147,300

22. Do not use commas in year numbers, page numbers, house or room numbers, telephone numbers, serial numbers (for example, invoice, style, model, or lot numbers), and decimals.

1973   8760 Sunset Drive   846-0462

The Semicolon

1. When a coordinating conjunction (*and, but, or,* or *nor*) is omitted between two independent clauses, use a semicolon—not a comma—to separate the clauses.

The estimated advertising expenses were high; the actual costs were low.

a. Use a semicolon to achieve a stronger break between clauses than a comma provides.

All of us are convinced that we will complete the project well before the end of next year; but no one is willing to guarantee that the final cost will be within the budget.

b. Use a semicolon when one or both clauses contain internal commas and a misreading might occur if a comma were also used to separate the clauses.

Craig Mach, the senior computer programer, enjoys his work; and his supervisor believes that this contributes to the quality of Craig's work.

2. When independent clauses are linked by transitional expressions, use a semicolon between the clauses. (If the second clause is long or requires special emphasis, treat it as a separate sentence.)

The bid was the lowest we could make; *however,* it was not low enough.

3. In general, when two independent clauses are linked by a transitional expression such as *for example* (abbreviated *e.g.*), *namely,* or *that is* (abbreviated *i.e.*), use a semicolon before the expression and a comma afterward.

He is highly qualified for the job; *for example,* he has had ten years' experience in the field.

4. Use a semicolon to separate items in a series if any of the items already contains commas.

The members of the panel were Elaine Osgood, executive vice president; Donald Berkowitz, marketing director; Cynthia Lindstrom, advertising manager; and Paul Hingle, sales promotion manager.

5. Use semicolons to separate a series of parallel subordinate clauses if they are long or contain internal commas. (However, a simple series of dependent clauses requires only commas, just like any other kind of series.)

She suggested that we should review the existing specifications, costs, and sales estimates for the project; that we should

analyze Bartlett's alternative figures; and that we should prepare a detailed comparison of the two proposals.

The Colon

1. Use a colon between two independent clauses when the second clause explains or illustrates the first clause and there is no coordinating conjunction or transitional expression linking the two clauses.

> **Last year was the worst in our company's history: profits were down 50 percent.**

2. Place a colon before such expressions as *for example, namely,* and *that is* when they introduce words, phrases, or a series of clauses anticipated earlier in the sentence.

> **The secretary of the committee has three important duties: *namely,* to attend all meetings, to write the minutes, and to send out notices.**

3. When hours and minutes are expressed in figures, separate the figures by a colon, as in the expression *8:25.*

4. A colon is used to represent the word *to* in proportions, as in the ratio *2:1.* (No space precedes or follows this colon.)

5. In business letters, use a colon after the salutation. In social letters, use a comma or no punctuation at all.

The Dash

1. Use the dash to set off a nonessential element that requires special emphasis.

> **It is your responsibility to educate our sales representiatives—as well as their supervisors—about the new health insurance program.**

2. Use a dash to show an abrupt break in thought or to set off an afterthought.

> **Here's gourmet food in a jiffy—economical too!**

3. Use dashes to set off single words that require special emphasis.

> **Travel—that's all he lives for.**

4. Use dashes to set off and emphasize words that repeat or restate a previous thought.

> **Right now—at this very moment—our showrooms are crammed with bargains.**

5. Use a dash before such words as *these, they,* and *all* when these words stand as subjects summarizing a preceding list of details.

> **Creative, ambitious, and personable— these are the qualities that I am looking for in a sales promotion manager.**

Parentheses

1. Use parentheses to enclose explanatory material that is independent of the main thought of the sentence.

> **Representative Vitale (D., New York) is interested in having us relocate in her district.**

2. Use parentheses to set off references and directions.

> **Since our expenses to date have been unusually heavy (see the financial report attached), we must curtail our spending for the rest of the year.**

3. Dates that accompany a person's name or an event are enclosed in parentheses.

> **J. P. Morgan (1837–1913) was a great financier and art collector.**

4. Use parentheses to enclose numbers or letters that accompany enumerated items within a sentence.

> **We need the following information to complete our order: (1) the list price of**

this product, (2) the minimum quantity that must be ordered, and (3) the credit terms available.

Quotation Marks

1. Use quotation marks to enclose a *direct quotation,* that is, the exact words of a speaker or a writer.

"Please have the marketing study ready by next month," said Ms. Campbell.

2. When only a word or phrase is quoted from another source, place quotation marks around only the words *taken from the original source.*

Miss Como said she would decide when she had "all the facts." (Miss Como's exact words were, "I will decide when I have all the facts.")

3. Words used humorously or ironically are enclosed in quotation marks.

It's "genuine" all right—a genuine imitation!

4. Slang or poor grammar that is purposely used is enclosed in quotation marks.

Whatever the secret may be, Jeff "ain't sayin'."

5. Words and phrases introduced by such expressions as *so-called, marked, signed,* and *entitled* are enclosed in quotation marks.

The letter was marked "Special Delivery."

6. Use quotation marks around titles that represent only *part* of a complete published work—for example, chapters, lessons, topics, sections, parts, tables, and charts within a book; articles and feature columns in newspapers and magazines; and essays, short poems, lectures, and sermons.

The section called "Effective Language" is very confusing.

7. Use quotation marks around the titles of *complete but unpublished* works, such as manuscripts, dissertations, and reports.

Please order a copy of Homelka's study, "Criteria for Evaluating Personnel."

8. Use quotation marks around titles of songs and other short musical compositions and around titles of television and radio series and programs.

Every year we end our New Year's Eve by singing "Auld Lang Syne."

9. A quotation within another quotation is enclosed in single quotation marks.

"Once again, this style is 'in' in the fashion world."

10. *Periods* and *commas* always go *inside* the closing quotation mark.

Mr. Ruffini said, "I don't understand the last paragraph."

The Underscore

1. A word referred to as a word is usually underscored (or italicized in print), but it may be enclosed in quotation marks instead. A word referred to as a word is often introduced by the expression *the term* or *the word.*

The words accept and except are often confused. (ALSO: The words "accept" and "except" are often confused.)

2. In a formal definition the word to be defined is usually underscored and the definition is usually quoted.

The term psychosomatic has an interesting derivation: the prefix psycho means "of the mind"; the root word soma refers to the body.

3. Underscore foreign expressions that are not considered part of the English language. (Use quotation marks to set off the translations.)

A faux pas literally means a "false step."

4. Underscore titles of *complete* works, such as books, pamphlets, long poems, magazines, and newspapers. Also underscore titles of movies, plays, musicals, operas, long musical compositions, paintings, and pieces of sculpture.

His new book, Office Management, is rather dull.

The Apostrophe

1. The apostrophe is used to form the possessive of nouns and certain pronouns.

employee's record   one's choice

2. The apostrophe is used to indicate the omission of a letter in a contraction.

doesn't   we're

3. The apostrophe may be used to form the plural of letters, figures, symbols, etc., if the plural might otherwise be confused. If no confusion will result, the apostrophe is unnecessary.

PTAs   1900s   BUT: dotting the i's

4. The apostrophe is used to indicate the omission of the first part of a date.

class of '80

CAPITALIZATION

1. Capitalize the first word of (**a**) every sentence, (**b**) an expression used as a sentence, (**c**) a quoted sentence, and (**d**) an independent question within a sentence.

The estimates were too low.

So much for that. Really? No!

The president said, "These statistics are inaccurate."

The question is, Will this policy improve employee moral?

2. Capitalize the first word of each item displayed in a list or an outline and the first word of each line in a poem. (Always follow the style of the poem itself, however.)

3. Capitalize every proper noun, that is, the official name of a particular person, place, or thing. Also capitalize adjectives derived from proper nouns.

George (n.)   Georgian (adj.)

South America (n.)   South American (adj.)

4. Capitalize imaginative names and nicknames of particular persons, places, or things.

the First lady   the Windy City

5. Capitalize a common noun when it is an actual part of a proper name. However, do not capitalize the common-noun element when it is used in place of the full name.

Professor Burke   BUT: the professor

the Chase Corporation   the corporation

6. Capitalize all official titles of honor and respect when the titles *precede* personal names.

Professor Ella McCann   Dr. Morgan

Mayor Pat Loo   Ambassador Franklin

7. In general, do not capitalize titles of honor and respect when they *follow* a personal name or are used *in place of* a personal name.

Dr. Arthur Orwell, *president* of Cromwell University, will speak tonight at eight. The *president's* topic is . . . .

8. Capitalize words such as *mother, father, aunt, uncle,* etc., when they stand alone or are followed by a personal name.

I called *Mother* and *Dad* last night.

9. Capitalize the names of companies, associations, societies, independent committees and boards, schools, political parties, conventions, fraternities, clubs, and religious bodies. (Follow the style used by the organization in its letterhead or other written communication.)

the Anderson Hardware Company

the Young Women's Christian Association

10. Common organizational terms such as *advertising department, manufacturing division, finance committee,* and *board of directors* are ordinarily capitalized when they are the actual names of units within the writer's own organization. These terms are not capitalized when they refer to some other organization, unless the writer has reason to give these terms special importance or distinction.

The *Board of Directors* will meet on Thursday at 2:30. (From a company memorandum.)

BUT: Edward Perez has been elected to the *board of directors* of the Kensington Corporation. (From a news release.)

11. Capitalize *the* preceding the name of an organization only when it is part of the legal name of the organization.

The Investment Company of America

12. Capitalize the names of countries and international organizations as well as national, state, county, and city bodies and their subdivisions.

the Republic of Panama

the Ohio Legislature

13. Capitalize short forms of names of national and international bodies and their major divisions.

the House (referring to the House of Representatives)

14. Capitalize *federal* only when it is part of the official name of a federal agency, a federal act, or some other proper noun.

the *Federal* Reserve Board

BUT: . . . subject to federal, state, and local laws.

15. Capitalize the names of places, such as streets, buildings, parks, monuments, rivers, oceans, and mountains. Do not capitalize short forms used in place of the full name.

Fulton Street	**BUT: the street**
Empire State Building	**the building**

16. Capitalize the word *city* or *state* only when it is part of the corporate name of the city or state or part of an imaginative name.

Kansas City **BUT: the city of San Francisco**

New York State is called the Empire State.

17. Capitalize *north, south, east, west,* etc., when they designate definite regions or are an integral part of a proper noun.

in the North	**the far North**
out West	**the West Coast**

18. Capitalize such words as *Northerner, Southerner,* and *Midwesterner.*

19. Capitalize *northern, southern, eastern, western,* etc., when these words pertain to the people in a region and to their political, social, or cultural activities. Do not capitalize these words, however, when they merely indicate general location or refer to the geography or climate of the region.

Eastern bankers	**BUT: the eastern half of Pennsylvania**
Southern hospitality	**southern temperatures**

20. Capitalize names of *days, months, holidays,* and *religious days.*

Wednesday   February

21. Capitalize the names of the seasons only when they are personified.

Come, gentle Spring.

BUT: Our order for *fall* merchandise was mailed today.

22. Capitalize the names of historical events and imaginative names given to historical periods.

the American Revolution

the Middle Ages

23. Do not capitalize the names of decades and centuries, such as *the thirties* and *the twentieth century.*

24. Capitalize formal titles of acts, laws, bills, and treaties, but do not capitalize common noun elements that stand alone in place of the full name.

the Social Security Act   BUT: the act

25. Capitalize the names of races, peoples, tribes, religions, and languages, such as *Chinese* and *Sanskrit.*

26. Do not capitalize the words *sun, moon,* or *earth* unless they are used in connection with the capitalized names of other planets or stars.

The *sun* was hidden behind a cloud.

The *Earth's* nearest neighbors are Venus and Mars.

27. Capitalize the names of specific course titles. However, do not capitalize names of subjects or areas of study, except for any proper noun or adjectives that are found in such names.

Black Literature 203 is a fascinating course. (Course title.)

His knowledge of *Black literature* is extensive. (Area of study.)

28. Do not capitalize academic degrees used as general terms of classification (for example, a *bachelor of arts* degree). However, capitalize a degree used after a person's name (Susan Howard, *Doctor of Philosophy*).

29. Capitalize trademarks, brand names, proprietary names, names of commercial products, and market grades. Do not capitalize the common noun following the name of a product.

Ivory soap   Westinghouse toaster

30. Capitalize all trade names except those that have become clearly established as common nouns.

Coca-Cola   Coke   Teflon   BUT: nylon

31. Capitalize a noun followed by a number or a letter that indicates sequence. **EXCEPTIONS:** The nouns *line, note, page, paragraph, size,* and *verse* are not capitalized.

Act 1   Class 4   Lesson 20   Policy 3948

32. In titles of literary and artistic works and in displayed headings, capitalize all words with *four or more* letters. Also capitalize words with fewer than four letters except (**a**) articles (*the, a, an*), (**b**) short conjunctions (*and, as, but, if, or, nor*), and (**c**) short prepositions (*at, by, for, in, of, off, on, out, to, up*).

How to Succeed in Business Without Really Trying

"Land Development Proposal Is Not Expected to Be Approved"

NUMBERS

There are two basic number styles in wide use: the *figure style* (which uses figures for most numbers above 10) and the *word style* (which uses figures for most numbers above

100). The figure style is most commonly used in ordinary business correspondence. The word style is used in executive-level correspondence and in nontechnical material.

Figure Style

1. Spell out numbers from 1 through 10; use figures for numbers above 10. This rule applies to both exact and approximate numbers.

> **He typed *ten* letters today. He usually types *one* or *two* a week.**

> **Please send us *35* copies of your bulletin.**

NOTE: Even the numbers 1 through 10 may be expressed in figures (as in this sentence) when emphasis and quick comprehension are essential. This is the style used in tabulations and statistical matter.

2. Use the same style to express *related* numbers above and below 10. (If any of the numbers are above 10, put them all in figures.)

> **Smoke damaged *5* dresses, *8* suits, and *11* coats.**

3. For fast comprehension, numbers in the *millions* or higher may be expressed in the following way:

> **21 million (in place of 21,000,000)**
> **14½ million (in place of 14,500,000)**

a. This style may be used only when the amount consists of a whole number with nothing more than a simple fraction or decimal following. A number such as *4,832,067* must be written all in figures.

b. Treat related numbers alike.

> **Last year we sold 21,557,000 items; this year, nearly 23,000,000. (NOT: 23 million.)**

Word Style

1. Spell out all numbers, whether exact or approximate, that can be expressed in one or two words. (A hyphenated compound number like *twenty-one* or *ninety-nine* counts as one word.) In effect, spell out all numbers from 1 through 100 and all round numbers above 100 that require no more than two words (such as *sixty-two thousand* or *forty-five million*).

> **James Edwards has interviewed *forty-four* people for the position of art director.**

2. Express related numbers the same way, even though some are above 100 and some below.

> **We mailed *three hundred* invitations and have already received over *one hundred* acceptances.**

3. When spelling out large round numbers, use the shortest form possible.

> **The Baxter Soap Company employs *eleven hundred* people.**

4. Numbers in the millions or higher *that require more than two words when spelled out* may be expressed as follows:

> **231 million (in place of 231,000,000)**
> **9¼ billion (in place of 9,250,000,000)**

5. Always spell out a number that begins a sentence, and for consistency, also spell out related numbers.

> ***Twenty-three* people attended each session.**

> ***Twenty* to *thirty* percent of the goods received were defective. (NOT: Twenty to 30 percent.)**

6. If the numbers are large (requiring more than two words when spelled out) or if figures are preferable (for emphasis or quick reference), rearrange the wording of the sentence.

Joe Carter sent out *364* letters. (INSTEAD OF: Three hundred and sixty-four letters were sent out by Joe Carter.)

7. Always spell out indefinite numbers and amounts, such as *a few hundred votes* or *thousands of dollars.*

Ordinals

1. Spell out all ordinals (*first, second, third,* and so on) that can be expressed in one or two words.

2. Figures are used to express ordinals in certain expressions of dates, in numbered street names above 10, and occasionally in displayed headings and titles for special effect.

NOTE: Ordinal figures are expressed as follows: *1st, 2d* or *2nd, 3d* or *3rd, 4th, 5th, 6th,* and so on. Do not use an "abbreviation" period following an ordinal.

Dates

1. When the day *precedes* the month or *stands alone,* express it either in ordinal figures (*1st, 12th, 23d*) or in ordinal words (the *first,* the *twelfth,* the *twenty-third*).

Her vacation starts on the *15th* of August and ends on the *30th* of August. (Figure style.)

2. When the day *follows* the month, express it in cardinal figures (1, 2, 3, and so on).

on March 6 (NOT: March 6th or March sixth)

3. Express complete dates in month-day-year sequence, such as *March 6, 1981.*

4. In United States military correspondence and in letters from foreign countries, the complete date is expressed in day-month-year sequence, such as *15 September 1981.*

5. In legal documents, proclamations, and formal invitations, spell out the day and the year. A number of styles may be used.

May twenty-first

nineteen hundred and seventy-six

6. Class graduation years and well-known years in history may appear in abbreviated form.

the class of '81

Money

1. Use figures to express exact or approximate amounts of money; for example, *$5; about $200.*

2. Spell out indefinite amounts of money; for example, *a few million dollars, many thousands of dollars.*

3. Do not add a decimal point or ciphers to a whole dollar amount when it occurs in a sentence.

His check for *$50* was enclosed.

In tabulations, however, if any amount in the column contains cents, add a decimal point and two ciphers to all *whole* dollar amounts for a uniform appearance.

4. Money in round amounts of a million or more may be expressed partially in words.

$12 million   OR: 12 million dollars
$10½ million   OR: 10½ million dollars

a. This style may be used only when the amount consists of a whole number with nothing more than a simple fraction or decimal following. An amount like *$10,235,000* must be written entirely in figures.

b. Express related amounts of money in the same way.

from $500,000 to $1,000,000

(NOT: from $500,000 to $1 million)

c. Repeat words like *million* and *billion* with each figure to avoid misunderstanding.

$5 million to $10 million

(NOT: $5 to $10 million)

5. Fractional expressions of large amounts of money should be either completely spelled out or converted to an all-figure style.

one-quarter of a million dollars
OR: $250,000

(BUT NOT: ¼ of a million dollars OR $¼ million)

6. For amounts under a dollar, use figures and the word *cents;* for example, *50 cents.*

a. Use the style *$.75* in sentences only if related amounts require a dollar sign.

Prices for the principal grains were as follows: wheat, $1.73; corn, $1.23; oats, $.78; rye, $1.58.

b. Use the symbol ¢ only in technical and statistical matter containing many price quotations.

The new prices for these items are as follows: lag bolts, 11¢; wood screws, 4¢; washers, 3¢; drill bits, 89¢.

7. When using the dollar sign or the cent sign with a price range or a series of amounts, repeat the sign with each amount.

$5,000 to $10,000   10¢ to 20¢

If the term *dollars* or *cents* is to be spelled out, use it only with the final amount.

10 to 20 cents

Measurements

1. Measurements that have a technical significance should be expressed in figures for emphasis or quick comprehension. Spell out measurements that lack technical significance.

This rate applies only to packages that weigh less than *2 pounds.*

BUT: I've gained another *two pounds.*

NOTE: Dimensions, sizes, and temperature readings are always expressed in figures.

This office measures *12* by *14 feet.*

2. When a measurement consists of several words, do not use commas to separate the words. The measurement is considered a single unit. The unit of measure may be abbreviated or expressed as a symbol only in technical matter or tabular work.

The shipment weighed only *20 pounds 6 ounces.*

I am *5 feet 4 inches* tall.

Fractions

1. A mixed number (a whole number plus a fraction) is written in figures except at the beginning of a sentence.

The cost of office supplies increased *2½* times this year.

2. A fraction that stands alone (without a whole number preceding) should be expressed in words unless the spelled-out form is long and awkward or unless the fraction is used in technical writing.

one-half the vote

three-fourths of the voters

3. Fractions expressed in figures should not be followed by *st, ds, nds,* or *ths* or by an *of* phrase.

3/200 (NOT: 3/200ths)

If a sentence requires the use of an *of* phrase following the fraction, spell out the fraction.

three-quarters of an hour (NOT: ¾ of an hour)

Decimals

1. Always write decimals in figures. Never insert commas in the decimal part of a number; for example, *665.3184368.*

2. When a decimal stands alone (without a whole number preceding the decimal point), insert a cipher before the decimal point. (Reason: The cipher prevents the reader from overlooking the decimal point.)

0.55 inch   0.06 gram

3. Do not begin a sentence with a decimal figure.

Percentages

1. Express percentages in figures, and spell out the word *percent.*

Spencer's Hardware Store was offering *20 percent* off any item.

NOTE: The % symbol is used only in tabulations, business forms, interoffice memorandums, and statistical or technical matter.

2. Fractional percentages *under 1 percent* should be spelled out or expressed in decimals.

one-half of 1 percent   OR: 0.5 percent

3. In a range or series of percentages, the word *percent* follows the last figure only. The symbol %, if used, must follow each figure.

Price reductions range from *20 to 50 percent.*   BUT: from 20% to 50%.

Periods of Time

1. In general, express periods of time in words.

a twenty-minute wait

in twenty-four months

2. Use figures to express periods of time when they are used as technical measurements or significant statistics (as in discounts, interest rates, and credit terms). Also use figures when the number would require more than two words if spelled out.

an 8-hour day   a note due in 6 months

Clock Time

1. Always use figures with *a.m.* or *p.m.*

a. The abbreviations *a.m.* and *p.m.* are typed in small letters without spaces.

b. When expressing time "on the hour," do not add ciphers to denote minutes except in tables where other times are given in hours and minutes.

Our store is open from 9:30 a.m. to *6 p.m.*

c. Do not use *a.m.* or *p.m.* unless figures are used.

this morning (NOT: this a.m.)

d. Do not use *a.m.* or *p.m.* with *o'clock.*

6 o'clock   OR: 6 p.m.

(NOT: 6 p.m. o'clock)

e. Do not use *a.m.* or *p.m.* with the expressions *in the morning, in the afternoon, in the evening,* or *at night.* The abbreviations themselves already convey one of these meanings.

at 9 p.m. OR: at nine in the evening

(NOT: at 9 p.m. in the evening)

f. The times *noon* and *midnight* may be expressed in words alone. However, use the forms *12 noon* and *12 midnight* when these times are given with other times expressed in figures.

The second shift ends at *midnight.*

BUT: The second shift runs from *4 p.m.* to *12 midnight.*

2. With *o'clock* use figures for emphasis or words for formality.

3. When expressing time "on the hour" without *a.m., p.m.,* or *o'clock*, spell out the hour.

> **He will arrive at *eight* tonight. (NOT: at 8 tonight.)**

With Abbreviations and Symbols

Always use figures with abbreviations and symbols.

$25   90¢   50%

No. or # With Figures

1. If the term *number* precedes a figure, express it as an abbreviation (singular: *No.;* plural: *Nos.*). At the beginning of a sentence, however, spell out *Number* to prevent misreading.

> **We have not yet billed the following invoices: *Nos.* 592, 653, and 654.**
>
> ***Number* 82175 has been assigned to your new policy.**

2. The symbol # may be used on business forms (such as invoices) and in technical matter.

ABBREVIATIONS

1. Use abbreviations and contractions sparingly.

2. Be consistent. Do not abbreviate a term in some sentences and then spell it out in other sentences.

3. When you do abbreviate, use the generally accepted forms. A number of abbreviations have alternative forms, with differences in spelling, capitalization, and punctuation. Again, be consistent.

4. In sentences, when a personal name is used, spell out all the titles except these:

SINGULAR	PLURAL
Miss	Misses
Ms.	Mses. (OR: Mss.)
Mrs.	Mmes.
Mr.	Messrs.
Dr.	Drs.

> ***Mr.* Ames will be the guest of *Professor* and *Mrs.* King.**

5. Abbreviations of academic degrees require a period after each element in the abbreviation but no internal space.

> **B.A.   Ph.D.   LL.B.**

6. The names of radio and television broadcasting stations and the abbreviated names of broadcasting systems are written in capitals without periods and without spaces.

> **Station KFRC   CBS officials**

7. The name *United States* is usually abbreviated when it is part of the name of a government agency. In all other uses, however, it should be spelled out.

> **U.S. Office of Education   OR: USOE**

8. Geographical abbreviations made up of single initials require a period after each initial but *no* space after each internal period. If the geographical abbreviation contains more than single initials, space once after each internal period.

> **U.S.A.   U.S.S.R.   N. Mex.   N. Dak.**

9. A few common business abbreviations are often typed in small letters (with periods) when they occur within sentences but are typed in all-capital letters (without periods) when they appear on invoices or other business forms.

> **c.o.d.   OR: COD   cash on delivery**
>
> **f.o.b.   OR: FOB   free on board**

10. Small-letter abbreviations made up of single initials require a period after each initial but no space after each internal period.

   a.m.   **p.m.**   **f.o.b.**

11. All-capital abbreviations made up of single initials normally require *no periods* and *no internal space.*

   RCA   **FBI**   **IQ**   **AT&T**

12. If an abbreviation contains more than single initials, space once after each internal period.

   loc. cit.   **op. cit.**

13. Each initial in a person's name (or in a company name) should be followed by a period and one space.

   Pat T. Noonan   **L. B. Anders, Inc.**

Index